AH

Pʀ

Making YOUR Teaching
Something SPECIAL

"*Making Your Teaching Something Special* is the book that I wish I had my first year of teaching. It is relevant to today's schools, and offers many quick and practical tips that can benefit new and seasoned teachers alike. The discussion questions at the end of each section are perfect to inspire reflection and dialogue, and can help us grow alongside one another as lifelong learners."

—**Sᴀʀᴀʜ Tʜᴏᴍᴀs**, educator and founder of Edumatch

"'May you inspire, and be inspired, each and every day.' In *Making Your Teaching Something Special*, Hurley does it again! He captures the attention of the reader with compelling and meaningful narrative. He weaves together personal experience and professional expertise with each section building upon the last. This is a must read for every teacher (PK–20)."

—**Mɪᴄʜᴀᴇʟ Lᴜʙᴇʟғᴇʟᴅ**, Ed.D., superintendent of schools, Deerfield Public Schools District 109

"Good teaching involves building positive relationships with students and their families. This book is loaded with great advice on how to improve children's lives. Whether you are new to teaching or a seasoned veteran, Hurley reminds us that teaching involves communicating and relating well with others, and his advice is useful in any type of teaching."

—**Rᴏɴ Sᴛᴀʀᴋᴇʀ**, librarian, Singapore American School, author of *Transforming Libraries*

"As a K–8 school principal, I believe that *Making Your Teaching Something Special* is a must-read for all teachers. Teachers' work is complex and with increased external demands, coupled with teachers' internal drive and commitment to improved professional growth, Rushton's concrete examples and perspective are sure to inspire and rejuvenate. Whether new to teaching or seasoned educators, all teachers would benefit from Rushton's comprehensive collection of relevant advice. The discussion questions that follow each unit can lead to meaningful professional conversations that are sure to make any school something special."

—**HADAR DOHN**, sager principal, Solomon Schechter Day School
of Metropolitan Chicago

"*Making Your Teaching Something Special* is the perfect companion to *Making Your School Something Special*. It goes without saying that teachers will find a plethora of gems in this second offering and, as in its predecessor, there is something for everyone who is determined to 'guarantee each year will be the best year of a teacher's career.' This is the top of my list as recommended reading for our instructional coaches, consultants, and the teachers they support in our teacher induction program and with all teachers in our school division.

"I really like the discussion questions, and these too will be a valuable resource for those supporting teams and developing the leadership capacity in our team leaders.

"Hurley colours his very practical and very real situations faced by teachers with great examples and pictures, taking the book beyond being a resource and into the realm of being a very enjoyable read. I really love his writing style and can literally hear him speaking as I am reading."

—**AUBREY PATTERSON**, superintendent,
Lloydminster Catholic School Division

"Rushton is on my short list of most inspirational educators, and his book does not disappoint. This book is a crucial read for new educators; his section on how to use extra, unplanned time at the end of class should be included in every teacher education program. However, Rushton also includes pieces important for more experienced teachers to read as well. Whether it is his take on extra credit, how we might rethink homework, or the importance of a pre-final, Rushton gave me a lot of things to think about and reflect on in my own practice."

—KARL LINDGREN-STREICHER, vice principal,
Westview Secondary School

"Learning is all about relationships, and students don't care what you know until they know that you care. Thank you, Rushton, for driving this idea home in *Making Your Teaching Something Special*. It's amazing how a few small changes in my behavior can make a world of difference for my students and the culture of my classroom. This book should be required reading for all preservice teachers, or any teacher looking to improve their practice or validate the awesome work they are already doing."

—DENNIS GRICE, instructional coach, digital literacy,
Concordia International School Shanghai

"The information and wisdom Hurley includes is very powerful. And I LOVE the concise style of writing! Too many authors (and many more students) feel the need to write more than is necessary just to fill space. The brevity of the chapters makes it easy to pick up when I have just a few minutes (I keep it in my purse at all times for this very reason). I believe it also makes it conducive to great professional development. It would be easy for staff members to read a chapter together and discuss within the time frame of a faculty meeting."

—SUMIKO CLARK, middle school teacher,
Walnut Creek Christian Academy

"In *Making Your Teaching Something Special,* Rushton Hurley condenses years of practical experience and acquired wisdom into an easily digestible how-to guide for novices as well as a crucial reminder for those old hands who may have fallen into a rut. In fifty (very) short chapters, he covers everything from lesson delivery to logistics, rapport with students to professionalism, and everything in between. This he does with the typical Hurley light touch and good humor.

"If I were in charge of a teacher training college, this book would be prescribed as an overview of the curriculum. Building your staff PD at your school, using this as the starting point, will also ensure that you stay focused on the things that really matter."

—**THEUNS OPPERMAN**, dean of academics,
Nova Pioneer Ormonde, South Africa

Making YOUR Teaching Something SPECIAL

50 Simple Ways to Become a Better Teacher

Rushton Hurley

Making Your Teaching Something Special

© 2017 by Rushton Hurley

These books are available at special discounts when purchased in quantity for use as premiums, promotions, fundraising, and educational use. For inquiries and details, contact the publisher: edtechteam.com/press.

Published by EdTechTeam Press
Cover design by Genesis Kohler
Editing and Interior Design by My Writers' Connection

Paperback ISBN: 978-1-945167-36-2
eBook ISBN: 978-1-945167-37-9
LCCN: 2017943595

Irvine, California

CONTENTS

You Have the Power to Change the World

Anyone who believes he or she doesn't have the power to change the world is wrong. Meaningful work is a goal for everyone, and every career has components that, to one degree or another, allow one to make a difference somewhere it is needed. Educators, however, occupy a special place in the realm of optimism. They enter the field because they believe they have something powerful to share and a confidence that what they teach can bring hope and possibilities to their students.

With that belief and confidence, teachers work to develop a wide-ranging command of the subjects they teach, take classes in instructional design and child psychology, and satisfy no small amount of government paperwork to become credentialed. Upon becoming certified and moving into the classroom, a gazillion little things pop up and threaten to derail heartfelt efforts to improve children's lives: abominable student behavior, combative parents, and mixed messages from leadership, to an ongoing lack of resources, disrespect from others in the community, a reminder every payday of how little society values schools, and (of course) no end to the government paperwork that started in the credential program.

Still, all the personal, professional, and psychological exhaustion and all the challenges that come from pushing yourself to be an effective teacher are offset when you see the students in your care begin to believe in themselves. It's great knowing that your work is meaningful to others, and it's even better to know that you, too, are improving even as you bring hope and possibility to light for others.

This book is for every teacher and teacher-to-be who believes (or is willing to be convinced) that educational, personal, and professional improvement come through effort, care, and experimentation. Bettering yourself and sharpening your skills make for a never-ending and incredibly rewarding process. As you progress through your career with that philosophy pushing you, you'll begin to understand something important about your chosen profession:

***Every year can be the best of your teaching career,
if you constantly improve.***

You'll find in these pages a collection of ideas and pieces of advice that come from the experiences many friends who teach and I have had in our own careers as educators. My hope is that what you and I explore together in this book will give you that extra something one of your students needs to be successful.

As I have spent most of my career working in middle and high schools, many of my stories will center on those settings. In almost every chapter, though, I believe the ideas will provide possibilities for those teaching younger students, as well as also those in colleges and training programs.

I have divided the book into five areas of teachers' experiences, each of which plays a part in shaping an educator's success:

- Rapport with Students
- Assignments and Assessments
- Delivery of Instruction
- Collegiality and Professionalism
- Logistics

Each area finishes with questions and activities for those using the book as part of a professional development plan. I think breaking out of the easy isolation that happens in our system is a necessary point of departure for personal and professional improvement, and I owe the idea for building these sections into the book to the kind critique of my friend Hall Davidson of Discovery Education. Credit where credit is due, always!

Some topics overlap between this book and my first, *Making Your School Something Special*. I believe that schools go from good to great partly as a function of making learning activities powerfully memorable, and I explore a number of ways teachers can do this in detail in that book. *Making Your School Something Special* focuses on what individual and team improvement can mean for the larger school community, whereas *Making Your Teaching Something Special* presents ideas and suggestions specific to each teacher's efforts to improve as an educator. Together, I hope these books empower professional educators to create the kinds of classrooms and school environments that allow children to thrive personally and academically, and adults to thrive personally and professionally.

One joke about teaching goes this way: "Teachers deserve a lot of credit. If their salaries were higher, though, they wouldn't need it."

Those of us who sought out the teaching profession aren't in it for the money. (Although we'd never turn down a raise!) What truly makes this work rewarding is the kindling of confidence, the power of possibilities, and the appreciation coming from connection and dedication that make the profession something special. Making any or all of that happen, though, requires more than just knowing one's subject matter.

It is my hope that what you find in this book will allow you to develop the extra professional and interpersonal insights and talents to make your work what one might describe as teaching at its highest levels. Take what is here, try it out, tweak and build upon it, and share with colleagues near and far what you discover. The ideas you pass along may enrich the lives of hundreds or thousands of others.

Perhaps you'll even write a book.

AREA 1

Rapport with Students

Chapter 1

Learn Their Names, Right Away

"But I'm terrible at names! My little brother was in kindergarten before I got his name down."

Remembering names is less like your height and more like the quantity of ice cream you choose for dessert. You have some control over the matter, and it may seem, at times, that doing it well (whatever "it" happens to be) is difficult, but there is always room to improve.

Let's be clear on why learning students' names *quickly* is important to do. Students' learning is as much about how they perceive you as it is what you do, and the better everything starts, the easier it will be for them to come into your classroom with an open mind and a good attitude about being there.

This is especially true if a student has more than one teacher and you're the first one to bother greeting him or her by name.

What if you're one of those people whose previous strategies for addressing students included calling out a really common name just to see who turns their heads? Is there anything you can do to get better at the name-remembering game? Absolutely.

On the first day, ask students their names as they arrive, and in your head keep repeating the names of those you've met as you wait to get things started. You won't get them all at this point, of course, but that intentional mental repetition does get you off to a good start.

When class kicks into gear, tell the students you will try to learn their names as quickly as you can, but that you expect to make plenty of mistakes the first couple of weeks. Your students, who are likely nervous about mastering what you will teach, will appreciate hearing the message that you know it can take time to learn something new.

Let them know that it is okay to help you, perhaps giving them a fun phrase to allow them to not have to correct you directly, which may be culturally difficult for some. The fun phrase could be anything: "I hope it's sunny today," for getting the name wrong, or "Great hairdo!" for a mispronunciation, or whatever you think might generate a smile on their faces.

Have activities that get them to be active a couple of minutes at a time, as well. While they pair up to learn something about each other or share what they know about one of the introductory vocabulary terms, keep repeating their names in your head. If you can't remember a student's name, tap that person on the shoulder and say, "Could you tell me your name again?" Once they tell you, say it again while looking at the student, and then smile, letting him or her know that you'll get it soon.

In the classes that follow, greet the students as they come in with things like:

"Michael, right? Good to see you!"

"Trinh, yes? How's your day so far?"

"Jenny, correct? Oh, it's Jane? All right, help me remember it. I'm glad you're here!"

Calling on the students whose names you are having the most trouble with can help you get those names more quickly, too.

Another approach is to have students do an activity in which they learn each other's names and report to the class something that isn't related to what you're learning. In threes, for example, one might say, "This is Nobu, and his hobby is reading. This is Juana, and she likes volleyball." As they practice, each student is working on two other names, and is benefiting from hearing the others repeat each one.

When doing this, choose a topic such as favorite foods or sports that isn't likely to exclude anyone, and do what you can to avoid those that could generate anything creepy. Also stay away from things people don't like, as it can be used as a proxy for tossing out something insulting or bullying. An activity like this means you (and everyone else) will hear each student's name at least twice, which is good practice for you and can help them feel more connected to the group.

One of my favorite professors in college, Dr. Don Clark, had a clever way of getting names down. He would end the first class by having students stand in groups of four holding white sheets of paper, and taking a picture of each group. He'd get prints of these (no digital options at that time) and write students' names where the paper appeared in the pictures. His office wall had several groups of pictures where he could get plenty of practice going over the names the first couple of weeks.

There are other, more involved techniques for learning names but for me, creating as many opportunities as possible for running through them in my head again and again seems most effective. Do whatever works for you; the more you work at it, the easier it will get, and the more your students will appreciate you for caring enough to know them by name.

Chapter 2

Don't Believe Everything You Hear

"Oh, you've got James in your class this year? Good luck with him. What a nightmare he was in my class!"

It could be that the teacher who makes such a comment about a "nightmare" student has tried everything humanly possible to connect with or reach the child, only to discover that "James" is possessed by a demon that no act of kindness or depth of care could exorcise.

But I wouldn't bet on demonic possession or any other scenario that assumes the child in your charge is truly and completely unreachable.

It is at least as likely that, early in the year, the teacher offering the warnings got into some kind of personality conflict with the student. Week after week, a sarcastic comment or judgmental facial expression taught James that nothing was going to go well with that teacher, so there was no need to try acting differently.

This is not at all to say that James didn't contribute to the situation. He may have been disrespectful in any number of ways, he may have been mean to other students, and he may well have made it difficult for those around him to learn. A response to such behavior is appropriate, of course, but sarcasm and unending disapproval may also be what sapped his hope that there is something to be gained by acting differently.

You can never truly know what lies behind a child's bad behavior. The situation at home may be horrible, or there may be pent-up disappointment, or grief, or frustration at always being treated as hopeless. Whatever the source of pain that is building walls around the kid's heart, it can take months or years of care to break it down.

If the year has begun, and you can see that a student like James is going to be a challenge for you, go find something positive about him from anyone who will share it. That may arm you to have a conversation like this:

"Hey James, before you go, there's something I want to tell you."

"Huh? What for? Am I in trouble?"

"Nope. I just want you to know that I heard from one of your former teachers that you have a strong creative streak in you. I feel like I'm seeing it, too, and wanted to tell you. That's all; see you tomorrow."

Chances are good this isn't the kind of message James is used to hearing. It probably won't result in a dramatic change then and there, but even a few kind, positive words can plant a seed of hope. If you keep encouraging him, even when reprimanding him, you may just put a crack in that wall.

"Hey James, let's focus, okay? I'm looking for you to live up to that potential you have!"

Whether it's you or the next teacher or the next who sees James turn around, the process has to start somewhere. As the teacher of the moment, you have the potential to set that process in motion.

Chapter 3

Talk With Rather Than At

Young people get talked at all the time. Statements, imperatives, directives, judgments, insults, and more come from those they live with, those they learn with, and those who teach them. It's easy (and efficient) to talk *at* students. The real question is, are you willing to take the time to talk *with* them?

Giving children the hope that what they say and think matters starts by moving from statements to questions—real questions that wait for real answers.

The question "How are you?" for example, is typically offered as a somewhat interactive greeting rather than a genuine request for insight into someone's life.

Think of that uncle who responds to "How are you?" with a litany of each ache, pain, and boil he currently experiences. As he delivers his depressing medical report, you desperately listen for him to take a breath so you can squeeze in a question that might move the conversation in a less graphic direction. And if there is no break in the monologue, you may begin mentally paring down the list of things you thought you were about to get done. Regardless of the topic, you listen to your uncle, knowing that, at some important emotional level, he just needs to be heard.

Asking students how they're doing isn't an interpersonal foul, of course, but students in need may answer with "fine" or "good" when they are nothing of the sort.

Getting a bit more creative with your greeting may open avenues that tell you much more about how they truly feel about themselves at that moment.

Let's use Ms. Watson and José as an example.

Ms. Watson: "José, how are you doing today?"

José: "Pretty good, Ms. Watson."

Ms. Watson: "Tell me, what's the coolest thing you've seen since our last class?"

José: "Well, it was pretty cool to see Curry hit that last-second shot to win the game last night."

If Ms. Watson didn't already know that José likes basketball, now she does. She could also ask him to describe or recreate the shot ("Tell me about it," or, "How did it happen?"), which would likely yield another glimpse of the young man's personality.

For discussion purposes, let's assume José is a bit of a character in class, someone who isn't always on task. If so, the way he describes the shot may be quite animated.

Ms. Watson (with a smile!): "I have a feeling that the shot, as good as I'm sure it was, wasn't as interesting as the description you just gave."

It isn't a complex interchange, but it represents a nice moment. Over time, those nice moments add up. Each connection—each relational deposit—shows José she cares. She can leverage those deposits later when she needs to correct or redirect José, while still maintaining a positive, caring relationship.

Some of the students who concern you most may respond to the question from the other extreme.

Ms. Watson: "Megan, how are you doing today?"

Megan: "Okay."

Ms. Watson: "Just okay? What's the coolest thing you've seen since our last class?"

Megan (quietly and looking down): "I don't know."

Ms. Watson (quietly and bending down so that their faces are level): "Are you okay?"

Megan: "Yeah, I just can't think of anything cool."

Ms. Watson: "Well, some days are cooler than others. And just so you know, I think it's cool that you're one of my students."

Megan may let loose a word of thanks or may shuffle forward without a response. Just how much of an impact the nice message will have is an open question, but based on the possibility that it's the nicest thing Megan hears all day, it's well worth Ms. Watson's time to have said it.

Chapter 4
Use Little to No Sarcasm

Y ou probably have plenty of colleagues with sarcastic senses of humor. As educated adults, we have developed intellects which allow us to appreciate well-crafted satire.

Some students, too, may appreciate sarcasm, but many will not. If they fail to understand what you really mean, the misunderstanding may result in a wedge that could take you weeks or months to overcome.

It's worth keeping in mind that students have enough trouble understanding what we mean when we are teaching our content. Operating on the hope that they'll have no problem with sophisticated humor may be problematically naïve. There is little potential gain that's worth risking the use of sarcasm, particularly if the wit is in some way directed toward a student who, hurt by comments he or she doesn't understand, is made to feel ignorant or, worse, like the butt of a joke.

All of that said, helping students understand more complex interactions is part of what we do. Within a controlled environment, such as a discussion centering on a sarcastic exchange between two characters in a story, helping understand this type of humor may be of immense personal value.

Let's imagine we have two characters in a story, with one using sarcasm to belittle the other. The target may be clueless as to the actual purpose of the bully's statements. Pointing that fact out may be one way to help prepare students for the kind of bullying that happens on many campuses regularly.

Sarcasm is rarely used to encourage others—and encouragement is a key piece of our job.

Sarcasm is synonymous with words like *ridicule*, *scorn*, and *mockery*. It is a communicative form that is rarely used to encourage others. A key piece of our job is to encourage students. As such, we should choose our communication patterns with enough care to keep from doing more harm than good.

Chapter 5

Be Willing to Apologize in Front of Everyone

A PLAY IN THREE ACTS.

Act One

I clearly remember a moment from third grade (or maybe it was fourth). I don't recall my teacher's name or what we were doing that day, only that my teacher apparently thought I was doing something inappropriate. Whatever it was, that isn't what I was doing.

She came up behind me and gave me a whack on the backside. All attention turned to me, of course. I was stunned, as I had no idea why I'd suddenly been paddled. She reprimanded me for whatever villainy in which she assumed I was engaged. She later figured out that she'd made a mistake. When we let out for recess, she called me over after the others had left the room.

To her credit, she apologized. But even at age eight or nine, I knew there was something lame about embarrassing me in front of everyone and then admitting her mistake only after the others had left.

Act Two

Fast forward about twenty years to a time when I was teaching a Japanese 1 class and one of the students, we'll call her Kim, said something that really got on my nerves. I responded harshly and went back to teaching.

After a few moments, though, with guilt hanging over my head, I stopped what I was doing.

"Everyone, what I said a minute ago wasn't the right way for me to respond, and I want to apologize. Kim, I'm sorry."

She mumbled something about it being okay, and we went back to what we were doing.

Act Three

Fast forward again, six or seven years. Someone sent me a link to a blog post written about me by a former student who was in the class the day I made the apology to Kim. The blogger wrote about what an important moment it was for him to see an adult apologize to a teen. Apparently that kind of interaction was a long way from normal in his experience growing up.

We do all kinds of little things that make a much greater impact than we imagine, both positive and negative.

You'll have moments when you say things in front of students you probably shouldn't. It happens. Be willing to make a genuine, public apology. It may be the most important lesson someone in the room learns all year.

Chapter 6

Buy Yourself Time When Annoyed

I t is likely that you experience moments when one or more of your students gets under your skin. My advice? Pause and delay.

More specifically, take control of what happens and when.

Often, we want to squelch an issue as soon as it arises. One problem with immediately addressing something (interruptions or inappropriate comments, for example) is that the person trying to push your buttons and derail you may actually succeed. Acting without giving yourself time to think about the breadth of the situation could play into the hands of the perpetrator, or at the very least, keep you from making a calm, rational decision about how to handle the issue.

One element of taking control is to simply pausing and looking in the direction of the student or students causing the problem. This keeps you from looking as if you aren't in control. (Nothing positive will result from your losing—or appearing to lose—control of the room or yourself.)

"*Hmmm.* Clearly you have some thoughts, and I want to make sure I understand properly. I'd like to connect about it to keep you focused on positives and out of trouble, so stick around a moment after class, and we'll talk."

If the student goes along with this, then you just de-escalated the situation for everyone.

The student gets time to settle down to some degree. You have maintained calm, letting the rest of the class know that you're an adult capable of controlling a situation positively. You've let the group know that inappropriate comments may result in lost time not for the whole class, but for the offending person specifically.

Nothing positive will result from your losing control of the room or yourself.

And on a personal level, the delay in addressing the issue can allow you to do one of the most important things anyone managing a class can do: address a situation not with a statement, but with a question.

I recall teaching a class during which one of the students asked a question challenging the nature of an assignment, and not in the good way that showed thoughtful consideration about the underlying value. She simply didn't want what she saw as extra work.

So I explained why we were doing the assignment.

She responded by rolling her eyes and tossing out, "Whatever!"

I'll pause here to tell you that "Whatever!" represents a pet peeve for me. Dismissing what someone else has gone to the trouble to explain is both uncool and disrespectful. I had no interest in letting that be the end of it. My best course of action would probably have been to buy time as described above, but I didn't do that. However, I did manage to salvage the situation somewhat by responding with a question.

"Sometimes people say 'whatever' to imply that what the other person said was worthless. Is that what you meant?"

This was a fairly aggressive move on my part, and was dangerous in that she might have answered that this was exactly what she meant, making a difficult situation worse. Fortunately for me and everyone else, she responded with, "No."

I think we all knew she was lying, but I'd given her room to back away from the position in which she put herself. In that moment, I didn't need a massive show of force to put her in her place; I just needed to get us past an awkward moment.

"Okay, no problem. Let's get back to the lesson."

It all ended well, but it likely would have been a better move for me to have said something like, "Check in with me after class. If I haven't explained something well, I'm happy to try a different approach. My goal is for you to be the best you can be, but it's probably better right now for us to go on with the lesson." Doing that might have also allowed me to ask the student if everything was okay. As I mentioned in an earlier chapter, disrespectful behavior is often a symptom of something that the child is dealing with at the moment. Rather than simply proving myself to be the one in charge, had I paused and delayed, it's possible that I could have proven that I cared about her and what she had to say.

Pausing and simply looking the student's way can convey the message that something said was at or over a line. A quiet pause with a serious, thoughtful facial expression can also serve to remind the class who is in charge—all while buying you time to decide how to respond.

Students will sometimes say and do things that annoy you. That's natural. If you respond well, even the most irritating student behavior may, in the end, provide you with a chance to prove yourself. You'll certainly want to get to the end of the day and be pleased with how you handled things. Before you act, give yourself time to think about how to achieve the best possible outcome.

Chapter 7

Handle Discipline Issues Yourself, If Possible

Someone in your school's leadership is the go-to person for discipline issues. He or she has the final say on punishment, and everyone knows it. There will be moments when you need to turn to this person for help, but choose those moments carefully, because they can come at a cost.

Whenever you pick up the phone to call "the disciplinarian" to the room, you are sending the message to students that you cannot handle the situation or the misbehaving student yourself. It is one thing if a safety issue is in play. In that case, calling for help is exactly the right thing to do. If, however, a student is simply acting out or being defiant, sending the student away or calling for help may not be your best move.

One teacher colleague of mine was an early-to-school guy, and whenever students would show up late to class, he'd have them come in fifteen minutes early the next day for "extra study time." That saved filling out a referral form and meant the student wouldn't be tardy two days in a row.

If the student showed up a little late for extra study time, he'd have the student come in fifteen minutes early the next day, too. If the student was later than a couple of minutes or forgot, they were told to come in for extra study time the next two mornings.

Only if the student failed again to come in early would the teacher move the issue on via referral to an after-school, one-hour detention. He almost never needed to do it, as the students were better off playing by his rules than amassing a discipline record.

> There will be moments when you need to ask for help with discipline, but choose those moments carefully, because they can come at a cost.

What made his solution work is the level of organization he put into it. If a situation arose, he would add the student's name and the reason to his calendar so that he could remember who was due for extra study. Keeping a record of who earned extra study time, when (or how often), and why, meant that he could, if needed, tell a parent what was going on using specific dates and referring to specific issues.

"Your son was late to class on the fourteenth, but successfully came in early on the fifteenth. On the twenty-third, he used the F-word, which runs against the level of civility we expect from everyone. He came in the next morning late for his time with me, so I had him come in on the twenty-fifth early, which he did."

Most parents appreciate clarity and organized documentation. It's when they feel that punishment is arbitrary or without any productive element that they may take a more argumentative stance and, absent a clearly articulated reason for some punishment, I wouldn't blame them for pressing the issue.

Note that having students come to you before school also gives you a chance to ask how things are going with classes or what the student has been up to of late. Being another voice telling them to be organized about their studies isn't a bad thing, and having a greater sense of what students do with their time can create positive connections.

Discipline, done well, can be good for a student who may be having troubles that have nothing to do with school. The added communication can allow them to open up and be encouraged and/or directed to needed resources. Find a pattern that allows you to combine a respect for rules with care for the individual, and you'll end up doing your students and yourself a lot of good.

Chapter 8

Make Positive Phone Calls Home

When I taught in the classroom, I would ask my Japanese 1 students for contact information for their parents or guardians at the beginning of each school year. While I had access to what was in the student information system, I wanted something a little simpler I could turn to when I wanted to check in with a parent.

I also felt I might get something a little different from some of them than what our system had, given the way I asked for the information.

How did I ask for it?

"All right everyone, I'd like you to fill out this form that includes contact info for your parents. There may come a time this year when you're getting a lot of heat from your folks about something. If you come and ask me to give them a phone call saying something positive just to balance things out a bit, I'm happy to help you out with that. It may not get you out of trouble, but it can't hurt. Just make sure you're doing something positive with your work in this class so I'll have something meaningful to say."

From one perspective, calling home with something good to report is a rather stunning spin on how students typically view the experience of a teacher phoning their parents. Many students have only experienced one kind of phone call from school—the kind focused on disappointment or discipline concerns.

Unfortunately, it seems that teachers, in general, only call home when students are in trouble. Calling home when you need a parent's help getting a kid on the right path is not a bad move, but let's hope for the kid's sake that negative phone calls aren't the only kind that come from the school.

Parents who regularly get calls from the school about their child's poor behavior or deficiencies may start believing that the child isn't capable of doing well. If the parent then relays that belief to their child, either through their words or by simply implying it through disappointed facial expressions, the student may begin to believe he or she has no chance to succeed in school. At which point, the child may begin to wonder, why bother?

It is worth your time to try to make at least one positive phone call home for each student, each semester. The fewer students you have, the more often you might be able to work this in. Here are several reasons for calling home with good news:

- A child who knows you're willing to let the parent know when he or she does good work may be more motivated to do well.

- Conversations with a parent or guardian may help you understand important pieces of why a child acts in a certain way.

- Being more aware of conditions at home can help you select more effective (or less problematic) things to say as you try to encourage a student.

- Mentioning to a parent what is coming in the way of important assignments or tests may mean that they will echo your messages to students to be well prepared.

- Your kind words may be the first positive message the parents have heard about their child from a teacher in years.

If you were zipping through the bulleted items above, take time to read the last one again slowly.

Whatever the annoyances you may experience with your work, you have the ability to say something that could defuse a bad situation at a student's home, or even shift the momentum for a relationship between parent and child in a positive direction.

Is that possibility worth several minutes of your time? I think it is.

Chapter 9

Build a Sense of Community

Imagine that you are at a high school football game. It's homecoming, and the stands are full. Behind you, a kid with impressive vocal power yells out a single word.

"*Getsuyo-bi!*"

A small army of students around him responds loudly with, "*Kayo-bi!*"

The first student then raises his volume again, shouting, "*Suiyo-bi!*"

His chorus responds with building excitement, "*Mokuyo-bi!*"

Others in the area have turned to watch what is happening, marveling at the enthusiasm exuded in this mysterious ritual.

Somehow reaching yet another decibel level, the first student thunders, "*Kinyo-bi!*"

The delirious chorus now screams in response, "*Doyo-bi!*"

And then, in unison, Loud Teen and his band of screamers release a final and deafening word: "*Nichiyo-bi!*"

They immediately follow with rapturous celebration as if the home team had somehow managed to score two touchdowns at once.

The person next to you then utters something to the group that you don't understand, followed with, "Great job! You guys are awesome!"

"What was that?" you ask this man.

"Oh, those are my students in the Japanese language program here. They're great, aren't they?"

You're not sure how great they are, as you really have no idea what just happened, so you ask, "What were they saying?"

"They ran through the days of the week," comes the reply.

You then notice the shirts the students are wearing, which include in English, "The Silver Creek Thunderously Hip Japanese Language Program."

The man "you" were talking to was me in the 1990s. I did all manner of things to give my students the opportunity to connect with the Japanese language program. It was my hope that feeling like a part of something a little different might also motivate them to study harder.

Looking back on my early years of teaching, I can identify plenty of things I did that could best be characterized as somewhere between unhelpful and obviously bad. Building the idea of The Silver Creek Thunderously Hip Japanese Language Program, though, was one of the moves that turned out to be wildly positive.

Here's the good news: You don't have to teach something unusual to make a sense of community happen with your students.

It seems that many schools do everything they can to standardize the experiences from one class to the next. This consistency has some clear benefits. For example, a student can switch from one class to another taught by a different teacher without too much disruption in learning if both teachers are covering the same content.

One would hope, though, that schools don't carry ideas of standardization to the point that teachers feel they can't create a compellingly distinctive environment for their group.

On the assumption that you're not working as a content-delivery robot, how might you create the kind of environment that makes kids feel lucky to be there? Some of the answers are straightforward enough:

- You show kindness and caring.
- You take time to encourage students.
- You remain calm when they think you'll explode.
- You are organized and fair about your grading.
- You laugh, or at least smile, on a regular basis.
- It's clear to the students that you are happy to be their teacher.

That's all stuff that makes you the kind of person students like. You can take things to another level, though, with distinctive activities.

The kinds of things that build community require extra time and energy, but the payoff is worth the effort.

I'll run through some of the things I used to do, and if adapting them for your setting seems like a good idea, give it a shot, and please let me know how it goes!

First, give your program a name. For us, it was The Thunderously Hip Japanese Language Program. Clearly, I was the one who chose the word "hip." It's a great word that reaches back into a time when I was much shorter, and I like it. (If you disagree, I respect your right not to be hip in this regard.) Another teacher I know, Lisa Highfill, established a sense of community within her class of fifth graders, which she called the "Highfill Crew." She promoted that sense of connection by sharing the clever and cool things they did via social media using their @highfillcrew handle.

Second, make it clear that your students are part of something ongoing. Every year in the first few weeks of school, I took a picture of each class and hung an 11" x 17" print on my classroom wall, captioning it with the class period and school year. Kids would sometimes wander in during break, lunch, or after school to look at the pictures from previous years and identify friends, cousins, or siblings. It was a little thing, but it seemed to be important to the students.

A colleague once told me how smart she thought this picture thing I was doing was. I told her the truth: The success was entirely an accident. I didn't have any clear idea that those photos would become so important; it just seemed like a good idea at the time. It's that way with a lot of classroom successes; it's only when students show their enthusiasm that we realize we are onto something good.

Third, put together activities your group can enjoy. What we called the Japanese Language Cheering Section for the Homecoming Game was one example (we had pictures on the wall of that, too, by the way).

We also enjoyed a once-a-semester Sushi Day. On that day, I'd order several big plates of rolled sushi and set up lunch in my classroom. Students lined up to get a couple of the tasty goodies, along with some soy sauce and wasabi. They could get back in line as many times as they wanted, as long as there was still sushi to be distributed.

Sushi Day and the club t-shirts were made possible by the fundraiser we held each year. I'll admit that I hated taking time for something that often seemed crassly commercial, but the fundraiser (for which kids sold wrapping paper and holiday items) could bring in a few thousand dollars, which proved useful for our activities throughout the year.

Yes, the kinds of things that build community require extra time and energy, but I believe the payoff is worth the effort. In my own class, I saw improved student engagement and effort, and fewer discipline problems. Not bad things, those.

Chapter 10

Attend Students' Games and Events

Are some of your second graders involved in an after-school drama program? If so, when the play happens, attend it.

Are some of your middle school students on sports teams? If so, try and attend at least one of their games each season.

Are some of your high school students involved in service efforts? If so, when they need chaperones or volunteers for their events, try taking time to join in.

It's hard to overemphasize how much your presence and active involvement can mean to students, particularly if they know that you were not required to be there.

The personal reasons for going to student activities are probably clear: Your students appreciate it when you take your time for them. If there isn't someone in their family who can show up to support them (or who has an interest in doing so), then knowing they have someone in the audience who cares enough to show up for them can be a huge emotional boost.

Attending these events might also yield some beneficial discoveries regarding your students' academic lives. For example, seeing how they interact with others, how they react to challenges, what they say at the event, and what talents they show may give you reference points when they are faltering with their work or behavior in the classroom.

Encouragement is not merely what you say, it's what they hear. A student may be more willing to listen if they know you're someone who has shown you will invest your time for them.

A young teacher, already busy trying to keep up with a teacher's workload, may respond to this idea in this fashion: "You want me to take my Friday night to go see a student's game? Look, I need a break from school, and besides, I have a date!"

Fair enough. We all need a break from what we do for our students. But it is quite possible that a date could actually learn something favorable about you by seeing you take time to encourage a student.

A friend of mine who has mentored teachers for years, Karl Lindgren-Streicher, related this story to me: "A student I had years ago who is becoming a teacher messaged me recently. She talked about how she went to a dance performance her students were in. They were so excited to see her there! She messaged me because she remembered seeing me at her performances and games and wanted to say thank you. It is particularly important for young teachers to go to games and performances—they'll be making enough mistakes that they need to bank some goodwill with their students."

Ultimately, you can learn more about someone from knowing how they spend their time than almost anything else. Be someone who gives time to others, as that is what most matters to most of those around us.

Chapter 11

Convey a Sense of Possibility

When I speak to an audience of teachers at a conference, I'll sometimes ask how long they've taught. "Raise your hands if you're in your first year of teaching," I'll request before going on to longer and longer periods of devoted service.

To those who raise their hands for the first question, I have a quick response:

"That's awesome that you're here! Just so you know, it gets better."

This message usually elicits a laugh, as everyone in the audience understands how hard the first year of teaching can be. It's my hope the message is one of encouragement: We made it through that hard initial experience, and they will, too.

Conveying that you know the process of learning to teach well is difficult can help the person in the middle of it find the courage to press on. In the same way, students need to hear that it is normal for the process of learning to be difficult.

As educators, we can never forget the time and effort it has taken to learn the content we teach. Yes, through our more extensive life and learning experiences, we understand that many fundamental concepts are relatively easy to master, but there isn't much to be gained by suggesting that to the students. Consider their reaction to your saying, "This part is easy."

If they have trouble with the content, they may believe you just suggested that they are stupid. I'm sure you don't actually believe that, nor would you ever intentionally convey that message, but remember that the way students respond to your teaching is more about what they hear than what you meant.

Learning new concepts can be difficult. What students need to know is that they can improve—just like a first-year teacher can get better at class management, insightful encouragement, and designing creative learning activities.

Some might protest, "Of course they know they can improve— they're students!"

While that would be nice, my suspicion is that there are many, many students who, over time, become convinced that they just aren't that good at one or more subjects. They simply hope to make it through the class somehow. They dismiss any success in those subjects as a fluke. This is what researcher and motivation psychology expert Carol Dweck calls the "fixed mindset." The opposite of a fixed mindset is the "growth mindset" which characterizes successful students who either instinctively know or have been encouraged to believe that they can learn new things.

For some of your students, knowing that you believe in their ability to learn is crucial in helping them develop a growth mindset. And they want—need—to know that you believe in them personally and individually.

Group encouragement like, "I know all of you can do this!" may leave the struggling student to assume you're talking about everyone else.

If you are talking individually with someone having trouble, however, the message cannot be so easily dismissed.

"Hey Jean, how are you doing with this?"

"Well, it seems pretty hard …"

"Don't worry; I felt the same way when I first learned these things. Have you had trouble with similar stuff before?"

"Yeah, when we first did this last year, I had no idea what my teacher was saying."

"Okay. We should just look at this in a different way. Seeing the other things you've done well with this semester, I know that once we find the right way to think about it, you'll be able to get it. Lots of students have trouble at first."

Knowing that you believe in their ability to learn is crucial in helping students develop a growth mindset.

This is no magic recipe for sudden confidence, but it is a message the student may need to hear from you.

You'll need, of course, to have other ways of describing the concept in question. If none comes to mind, then check with a colleague, as you are on the hook for following through with your optimism. Coming up with different ways of explaining what you teach may require plenty of patience, but getting the student to a point of confidence will provide something you'll be able to build on going forward.

Perhaps needless to say, the reverse will yield much more than the student missing an idea. Conveying any sense that you aren't able to help the student is likely to be interpreted by that student as personal failure, and that's baggage which will be brought to future topics.

The most successful team among the four most popular American professional sports, as measured by overall winning percentage over the last twenty years, is the San Antonio Spurs basketball team. The coach, Gregg Popovich, has a quote on the locker room wall (in multiple languages, I have been told) he uses to motivate his team to practice hard:

> *When nothing seems to help, I go and look at a stonecutter hammering away at his rock perhaps a hundred times without as much as a crack showing in it. Yet at the hundred and first blow it will split in two, and I know it was not that blow that did it, but all that had gone before.*

The quote is by photographer, writer, and journalist Jacob Riis, and is known as "The Stonecutter's Credo." Riis worked to help readers understand the plight of those living in New York City's tenements in the late nineteenth century, and his work is credited with the implementation of policies that helped many of the city's poor.

The Stonecutter's Credo just as easily applies to your work as an educator. You keep at it, conveying your sense of a student's possibilities, trying everything you can to get a student past her or his challenges until, finally, understanding settles in.

When it does, you've done more than teach your subject. You've given a child hope for the future, and your persistence won't be soon forgotten.

Chapter 12

Know You May Not Know What They're Thinking

Some years ago, I had a student in one of my third-year Japanese classes who had done well in her first two years, but started falling behind early that fall semester.

I reminded her many times that she needed to get her work done. She didn't.

I asked if she was okay several times. She said she was, though she didn't really sound like it.

She managed to make it through the school year with a passing grade, but her performance was a far cry from how well she'd done before.

Some months later, I learned from another teacher that the girl's father had passed away the summer before. Suddenly, the change she had exhibited made complete sense.

A number of discussion items arise from this example. We could discuss whether a teacher is responsible for factoring in life circumstances when assessing a student's performance. Or we might consider the potential for students to manipulate teachers who give any room when there is a personal story behind weak performance.

For me, the lesson I learned from this experience was about what efforts represent an effective check-in with a student when performance drops. It is here that I believe I failed my student.

Asking if someone is okay is not a bad move, but it may do little more than scratch the surface to reveal what is happening in the person's life. She and I might have been better served if I had asked, "Is there something going on that is the cause of your grade dropping? You just don't seem to be the same student you were last year, and I was wondering."

The real issue, of course, is not the grade, but the possibility that there is something happening in the child's life for which help is needed. If you discover that a student has lost a parent, for example, you might work with a counselor to find a resource for grieving kids.

Showing concern and reminding students that they are capable of doing well is clearly an important piece of teaching. But without a complete picture of what's going on in a child's life, we may make assumptions—that the child is simply lazy or has "senioritis"—that send counterproductive messages as we communicate verbally and nonverbally with our students. Rather than assuming that the child is lazy or lackadaisical, assume that other factors are in play if you see a notable change in a student's level of effort and engagement.

One of our primary jobs is to help students gain a command—hopefully a confident command—of the material we teach. Being a caring adult in their lives enhances our chances of doing this for any given student. And being a caring adult requires remembering that we may not know what is in a student's head and heart.

Discussion Items for
AREA 1: Rapport

In your team meetings or brainstorming sessions with colleagues, use the following questions to explore possibilities for strengthening rapport with students. As you come up with more questions that prove useful, please share them at tinyurl.com/MYTSS-suggestions.

1. Do you know a special technique for remembering students' names?

2. Do you have a student who has struggled in the past, but is now on the right track? What led to the improvement?

3. What is something that a student has told you that you know you will never forget?

4. Are there things you say that you think are funny, but you assume the students don't understand? If so, consider how they may think of you based on various interpretations of what you think is funny.

5. Have you apologized to a student in front of others?

6. Do you have pet peeves that are hard to set aside when you are teaching?

7. How would your students describe you in terms of fairness and discipline?

8. When was the last time you made a positive phone call or sent a positive e-mail to a parent? Which of your students most needs you to do that today or tomorrow?

9. How would your students describe the experience of being in your class? Do they feel connected to their classmates in some way?

10. What is the next student sports or extracurricular event you plan to attend?

11. What are unusual but effective forms of encouragement you have tried or seen?

12. Thinking of a student who is struggling, what do you assume is the cause, and what other issues may be in play that you haven't thought of before?

Area 2

Assignments and Assessments

Chapter 13
Give Options

Within two to three months of the start of the school year, and perhaps even earlier, most teachers have a pretty good idea of which students are the stars, and which are the challenges.

By "stars," I mean the students who do what you ask, contribute in class, and/or earn good grades. Other students are surely wonderful in other ways, but for the purposes of this item-o-advice, "stars" are those who learn and follow your directions without complication.

By "challenges," I mean those who aren't getting work done, aren't performing well on the assessments, and whose study habits seem to be somewhere significantly south of optimal.

It may well be that when you give a quiz or assign a project, you can predict with great accuracy who will do well and who won't. When you realize that you have this power of prediction, know this: It's a sign that you need to shift course.

I am not suggesting that the ones doing well need to be knocked down a notch or two. What I am suggesting is that your "stars" may have simply gotten into a groove in which it isn't all that hard for them to do what you've asked. Pushing them to explore new approaches to their learning can allow them to see and develop new talents.

At the other end of the spectrum, those who do poorly are probably not served by repeated failures that make them feel as if they can't achieve. Again, be careful here. I am not saying that you should imply that your "challenges" are being successful when they are not. As with your "stars," inviting the students who are struggling to explore a different approach to learning may help them succeed.

Let's say that you are about two weeks away from a quiz. You could address new possibilities with their studies in this way:

"All right everyone, we're about a week into this topic, and as you know, we'll have a quiz at the end of next week. If you would prefer not to take the quiz, but show your learning in some other way, you may do so, but you'll need to get what you have in mind approved by me no later than this Friday."

Some might think that this is designed to make it easy on those who aren't currently putting forth enough effort I'd certainly hope not, but that depends on you. I'd suggest following what's above with something along these lines:

"Whatever you choose will still have to show that you have a command of the different concepts we're working with, along with meaningful questions to where these ideas take us, and connections to other items you've learned."

Students who embrace this challenge may come at their preparations for their presentation, video, song, or whatever else, in a much more effective way than what they have done before, whether they are your "stars" or your "challenges." They may even do something you don't know how to do yourself. For example, let's say that you are offering those interested the chance to make a video instead of doing a set of slides related to some topic:

"Your slide presentations are due Friday of next week. Those of you who will do videos instead need to have your scripts approved by the end of this week, or I'll expect you to show up with slides. Also, if you need help making a video, don't come to me, as I have no clue. Find help from some good soul among your classmates or somewhere else on campus, or show up with slides."

Do those with good grades actually understand the material?

What really matters is that the students can articulate their understanding of what you teach and move those ideas in interesting directions. How they do it, for the most part, just isn't that big a deal.

Don't make the common mistake of confusing doing well on the assessments with actual learning. A truly professional teacher understands that assessments are often subject to the manipulation of clever students. It is perfectly possible that there are those in your class who have good grades, but who wield little understanding of the concepts covered. In other words, they are good at taking tests, but the information never really sinks in meaningfully. (See the wonderful YouTube video "Confessions of a Converted Lecturer" by Eric Mazur of Harvard for a detailed exploration of this phenomenon: tinyurl.com/mn6a7k7.)

Regularly ask yourself whether those with good grades understand what you teach, and whether those with bad grades don't. Be honest with your evaluation, be willing to change your approach, and give students options for how they can best demonstrate their understanding.

Options help you to figure out what kinds of assessments will allow students to push themselves. Doing this will both optimize their chances for success, and also continually expand your ability to figure out what your "stars" and your "challenges" need.

Chapter 14

Ask for Fascinating

It can be a tedious experience to see similar answers over and over and over. That repetition may be great if you are looking for the production of right answers, but it is somewhere between uninspiring and maddening if you're reviewing one long essay after another with little to no variance among the submissions.

Most students, and most adults, are geared simply to handle what's required. Doing the minimum may be a function of efficiency as part of a larger goal of addressing as many of the items on the overflowing plate as possible. When students do what you ask, and no more, the issue isn't necessarily that they are lazy. Rather, they want to accomplish what you have asked and move on.

Therefore, what you ask for may be the key to getting notably more interesting material.

As part of a project several years ago, I worked with a set of teachers, charging each group of four or five to come up with a set of geographic facts. In each group, one person created a shared slide presentation, containing one slide per person. Each then thought of whatever geographic fact they could pull from their consciousness at that moment and placed at the top of his or her slide.

One teacher came up with this fact: Grapes grow in Italy.

Is it true? Yes, and easily verified by those with an interest in liquids not served in the school cafeteria.

Next, I asked the teachers to go to the slides of the other members of the group, and on each one, add a question that followed from the fact. The follow-up questions that appeared on the slide with our grapes statement, above, were these:

- What else grows in Italy?

- What products come from grapes?

- Where else are grapes grown?

I stopped the group after giving them enough time to generate some questions, and asked if they had put at least one on each slide in their group's presentation. They confirmed they had.

I then asked, "Okay, are the questions you wrote [short pause for effect] fascinating?"

That was greeted with stares, followed by, "Give us another couple of minutes."

I did.

After another few minutes of work, the questions had a decidedly different look. The teacher with the "grapes grow in Italy" fact now had these questions on her slide:

- How is climate change having an impact on Italy's grapes, and how does this compare/contrast with other grape-growing regions?

- How do the winemakers create consistency in wine production?

- Have Italy's sales of wine been affected by the ever-growing popularity of Napa and Sonoma County winemakers?

Note that the second set of questions came from the same people, in the same place, doing the same activity, at almost the same time. The one difference is that the participants had been asked to make their work fascinating.

While wine production may not be the perfect topic for students, the bottom line is that you probably won't get fascinating work unless you ask for it. This simple request may result in something far more interesting for both the students as they work and for you as you assess their work.

Will the students respond with genuinely interesting ideas? Some will, and some won't. Still, when grading a number of assignments, having a few fascinating ones can carry you through without tedious frustration producing any self-inflicted harm.

Chapter 15

Maintain a Balance between Creating and Evaluating

At some point in the not-too-distant past (looking in the mirror, noting the gray hair, and choosing to move on), I can see myself as a student creating a poster and presenting it to my classmates. It wasn't a bad approach to sharing what we learned, and the posters benefited from being more active and definitely different than most of what we were doing in our classes.

Over time, posters gave way to PowerPoint presentations, which minimized the need for cardboard and tape, but assaulted us with bulleted blurbs both abominable and unbearable in their blandness. Yes, some teachers helped students learn to use the tool in a way that more effectively enhanced the presentations, but in my experience, such teachers represent a not-particularly-populous minority.

Today, a stunning variety of tools are available for inflicting presentations on one's peers and teachers. Whether the quality of presentations created with today's high-tech tools is any better than posters or PowerPoint is still open for debate. The reason? Presentations using cardboard, PowerPoint, or video (or perhaps holographic interpretive dance—I haven't seen one of these yet, but am thinking it may not be that far off) all tend to suffer from the same preparatory deficiency: Students are asked to create before meaningfully considering examples of varying quality.

The "varying" part in the last sentence is important. It's common for teachers to show their students one or two examples of exceptional work. But knowing what's good is different than explicitly knowing what to avoid.

Put simply, creating anything one can be proud of is easier if one has seen how others have approached the task in various ways. My nonprofit, for example, runs video contests several times each year that ask students to explain in ninety seconds or less something one might encounter in school.

Consider how a student would respond to the challenge to explain something, however. When they think of teaching something, often what pops into their head is someone standing at a board, talking at those sitting and listening. Making a video about this would therefore mean putting someone next to a board, putting another behind a phone pushing "record," and letting the explanation flow. After all, that's how they normally see teaching.

What's interesting about video, though, is that there are so many avenues for getting a thought across using images, art, screenshots, footage, etc. When students see videos taking quite different approaches to what they had in mind (see this stop-motion example of students explaining the breathing system at Nextvista.org/the-breathing-system), they are more likely to think along new lines.

Taking time to look at what others have done can lead students in constructive directions; seeing a variety of examples empowers them to create material of greater quality.

Staying with the video example, let's say you want to have students create videos that address topics you've put in front of them. The idea may be to create a set of videos that will be beneficial to them as they review the content from your latest unit and help students in the future as they work to become comfortable with the concepts.

Before having them create anything, have them evaluate what other students have done. Here's one way to do this: Provide a set of student-made videos. The large set of Next Vista contest-finalist videos is one with plenty of variety in approaches to telling stories of learning. As homework, direct the students to choose three or four videos in the set, making notes on the following for each of them:

- what you found strong and/or compelling about the video

- what you thought was weak or could be improved

- how you would have approached the topic differently (more than simply correcting weaknesses, this is about thinking of completely different approaches to explaining the topic)

In the next class, have them discuss what they found, and perhaps watch a few together that seem exceptionally strong or weak. The more they talk about weaknesses, the less likely they are to repeat the mistakes.

If you have a set of videos that cover the material you are teaching, you could also ask them to talk about what a given explanation might have missed, or how one would validate the information presented in the piece.

Even young students can benefit from learning to critically examine what they are shown. The language might be a little nicer ("Is there anything in the video that you think could be improved?"), but at core, we want to make sure that students have a variety of ideas to work with as they consider how they'll show what they've mastered and how they extend the ideas going forward.

We want students to create material that will be interesting and valuable. Making sure they spend time evaluating what others have done makes that all the more likely.

Chapter 16

Make Extra Credit Time Well Spent

Extra credit is a topic of wide debate. Some teachers love it; others loathe it. Rather than debate its intrinsic value here, I want to make sure that it is meaningful for the students—because so many teachers *do* allow students to earn extra credit.

As a teacher, there were only three reasons I provided an extra-credit opportunity related to homework:

1. I wanted it to help the students raise their grades.

2. I wanted it to help them strengthen their understanding of what they were learning.

3. I wanted it to help them develop better habits.

My grading system boiled down to one-third homework and two-thirds tests and projects. Remember that I was a Japanese language teacher. For me, getting the material in front of my students' faces as often as possible was a central goal.

I'll add that I rarely graded homework on its accuracy, preferring instead to see that they were doing lots of writing of the syllables and characters, and practicing common structures with sentences. With the more advanced classes, I also gave them regular opportunities to fashion their own assignment for working with the language. They could choose a default approach, or they could ask for my approval to create their own assignment (which I almost always gave).

Over the course of the term, though, some students would have days where they didn't get the homework done. Maybe it was a crunch time with other classes or athletics, or maybe they were having challenges at home. Whatever it was, I learned not to get upset when not everyone did the homework. Had I not learned that lesson, I'd have quit out of frustration early in my career.

Late in the semester, there would invariably be students who wanted to improve their homework percentage as we moved toward final exams. Here's how I'd introduce the opportunity:

"Alright everyone, next week is Thanksgiving break. Some of you need some more points to raise your homework average. Others want some extra incentive to start studying earlier for the end-of-term exam. Here's how it works.

"You normally get three points for a homework assignment. Earning back those points will cost you three times as much work as a regular assignment, but that will give you all the more practice as you review your topics, vocab, grammar, and characters. Feel free to do enough practice to earn back as many as twelve points."

I'd explain the mechanics of what they had to do, which, simplified for our purposes here, involved a substantial amount of work. Some students would look at me with facial expressions that suggested that doing that much for so few points wasn't going to happen.

I'd continue.

"This is purely optional, of course. Many of you are doing just fine with the material and your grades, and you don't need the extra points.

"However, if you get to the end of the semester, and your overall grade is an 89.4 percent, you may ask if I'll round that up to an 'A.' If you do, I'll look at you and say, 'Nope. But wow, if you'd only done a little of that extra credit over Thanksgiving, you'd have made it to an A.'

"So choose wisely, and know what the answer to that question will be should you ask it."

Getting the material in front of my students' faces as often as possible was a central goal.

I knew that many of my students had a tendency to procrastinate on preparing for their final exam. While the extra credit represented a lot of volume in terms of work to do, it also meant that they would get plenty of practice before they began the more exam-focused preparation. I explained this at the beginning of each term. And yes, it's possible that knowing there would be the opportunity to earn extra credit could have led some students to ignore the homework assignments they otherwise could (should) have done. By design, however, earning the extra credit meant they had to do three times the amount of work at a time when the review was especially helpful.

My approach to extra credit worked for some students, and didn't others, pretty much like everything else I did. Whatever your approach is, make sure you can explain the extra-credit grading system to students, parents, and colleagues. You should also be able to outline how it will help a student with his or her understanding of the material. If you can't, don't give it.

Chapter 17

Have Students Create Materials to Help Others

From the very first time my students used simple video tools to complete their projects, I knew something important had happened.

First, the quality of their work was much better than the projects we had done previously. Second, as we watched the videos, the students enthusiastically applauded each other's work. Their work was better, and they were celebrating the efforts of their classmates.

The video projects went over well for a number of reasons:

- Students had the chance to work with peers.

- They enjoyed the creative aspect of making videos.

- They knew there would be a wider audience for their work.

- They knew exactly what the audience would see.

- Videos are cool.

The first two items are easy to understand. Students often enjoy the chance to work on something with a friend, and the high fives they gave one another after their videos were shown suggested a pride in having accomplished something together.

The next two items regarding the audience turned out to be critical pieces of their motivation to produce strong work. Watching students fine-tune their work after school fascinated me. My guess is that most of the work I gave them didn't yield this determination to get their projects just right. Showing their videos to the class raised the stakes. Here's the reason: When students know others will see their work, they want it to be good. When it's just for the teacher, they want it to be good enough. The difference is important. Students who push themselves to make something really good, rather than simply acceptable, learn what they are capable of doing.

Students who push themselves to make something really good, rather than simply acceptable, learn what they are capable of doing.

The last item in the bullets above regarding "cool" also contributes to the interest in generating something strong. Simple effects can make a video fun to watch, and with so many free tools available to make videos look good, students can be reasonably confident that the class will enjoy what they create and share.

The teacher's main job is making sure that the fun of the video doesn't crowd out a meaningful exploration of the content they study. I learned to approve scripts before I'd let them start filming, as that would allow me to hold their feet to the academic fire as they leapt into their videos.

Students like making videos. And when their plans are gently guided and monitored, they can produce genuinely interesting and intellectually stimulating material. This truth is the philosophy underlying NextVista.org, the nonprofit I run: Students can create cool, short videos that help others grappling with the highlighted topics.

In your classroom, this reality can mean that what students create as projects for your class can form a creative bank of videos they—and the students who follow them—can repeatedly review as they study challenging concepts. For that matter, why not charge your students to push themselves to create great material for your classes so that, rather than creating the material from scratch yourself, you can focus your time on other efforts?

We all want to be able to draw upon compelling material to use in class. Clever videos made by others who are (or were) their age easily qualify as "compelling" for most students. Over time, as your library of student videos expands, you'll have a wealth of content to draw upon to share with future classes.

Chapter 18

Explore the Value of Your Assignments

The goal of every assignment is (or should be) to help your students learn something. From homework to classroom activities to projects, quizzes, and exams—every task or assessment is assigned for the purpose of helping students become comfortable with concepts and material in your curriculum.

Deeper learning may be your intention, but that doesn't mean your assignments always deliver the desired result. Obviously, not every student will master the content you put in front of them. But by consciously questioning the value and effectiveness of all of your assignments, you can ensure more meaningful learning for those who complete the work. From my point of view, this kind of intentional evaluation of the purpose and effectiveness of assignments is something we may not be doing often enough.

The most common target I've encountered in discussions of the value of learning activities is the math-problem set. Imagine a sheet of paper with fifty equations to complete. But what if doing ten would have been just as effective? Or, how about assigning five and requiring students to provide feedback in the form of a couple of sentences about what the student thinks is challenging when doing the problems?

It may not be all that different for writing. If you assign four essays over the course of the semester, is that meaningfully better than three? Should you have assigned five? If you can't easily convey and draw distinctions for the different goals for each of the essays, then doing another may not be yielding enough value for the student to merit their time spent doing it and your time spent grading it.

Another way to evaluate assignments is to consider this question: Are you giving students busywork? If what you're having them do is failing to help them move forward with their learning, then the assignment is simply filling time, and the answer to the question is yes.

Strong opinions about the role of homework abound. Some see a large volume as a reflection of a challenging curriculum, some see frequent practice as necessary for what they teach, and others think that homework hardly ever allows a student to make significant progress with the ideas in their classes. Few teachers check with the people who have the most direct sense of the value of homework: their students.

Engaging students in the question of what is most helpful for their learning runs the risk of the talkative ones taking the opportunity to push for simply doing less. The results of summative assessments, though, make for the teacher's ace in the hole. If students can do well on their assessments by doing different assignments, or even less homework, then not only are you meeting the core goal (students' successful learning), but you are creating an atmosphere in which students can learn to collaborate with you to determine what is effective. The bottom line is whether what you ask students to do results in learning. Being honest with yourself about the value of what you assign, and getting meaningful feedback on what you try, can make for a better, and notably more effective, classroom environment for everyone.

Chapter 19

Create Ready-to-Go Activities

W e all have moments in our teaching when something we planned takes less time than we thought.

I recall having times when I'd finished my lesson and had five to ten minutes left in the period. On those rare occasions, I encouraged my students to get a head start on the homework only to see otherwise perfectly good students respond by tossing their books into their bags and talking with each other as they awaited the bell. Rather than let those minutes be spent unproductively, I would have them get their work back out, hovering over them to make sure they at least went through the motions of getting something done—not tons of fun for them or for me.

A natural way to address such moments is to prepare ready-to-go activities that you can launch whenever needed. These are activities that would address the goals you have for your students and could fit in almost anywhere in the curriculum.

REVIEW ASSOCIATION

One activity is what we can call "review association." Rather than reviewing what you have taught before exactly as you taught it before, you can try putting some kind of prompt in front of them, and asking them to associate it with something you've covered at some point during the school year.

That association can be anything—a word, a quote, an image, a short video. In fact, trying all of these can be good for variety. The key is for students to practice drawing connections among concepts they've been studying.

Imagine you have been studying light waves and you play a short video of a car passing by, honking its horn. Without any further commentary, let the students begin to work with ideas.

They may have to figure out why the sound changes pitch as it passes, and that will remind them of the Doppler effect, or they may encounter the idea as they do a search on what they saw and heard in the video. They may then draw connections to similarities between light and sound waves.

Perhaps you have been studying the beliefs of the Aztecs. You put a picture of an elevator door in front of the students. That may lead to ideas about steps, which could get them to pyramids and the role of high priests standing on these structures, performing religious rituals.

What's important with exercises like this is to leave room for exploration and discussion; not having an obvious answer strengthens the activity. What students do with the prompt is up to them. I recommend having them work in pairs or threes, and then you can take time to circulate just to listen to the discussions. After several minutes, put ideas from several groups on the board, making it clear that you're not looking for any one answer. Give them another few minutes to try to associate something they discussed with another group's ideas.

You don't need to draw any connections yourself, and you may not even see any. Give them room to surprise you. All you need is to have some interesting quotes, images, etc., ready to go when you find yourself in a class with extra time.

ADVENTURE DESIGN

Another ready-to-go activity is "adventure design." Remember the choose-your-own-adventure books from back in the day? Get students to design components of a game that requires knowing something about what you've been studying. This activity gives students plenty of room to associate their own interests with what they're learning.

If enough interesting game ideas crop up built on the course content, you could even devote time in an upcoming class to having students actually create their adventure designs using hyperlinks in a Google Doc. Students can create a Doc with a scenario and three possible choices. Each choice can be linked to a new Doc that is either a game-ending piece or a new scenario. The new scenario should be a creative linking to what another student has done.

And sure, there's no guarantee that the groups will come up with concepts that work well together. But so what? The point is to find ways to keep asking questions about what the class has been studying. The game may end up being amazing—or a set of highly tenuous connections. Regardless, if students have been actively thinking through the content, you are probably better off than simply you would have been by simply letting them start the homework early.

RHYME TIME

A third activity you might try at a moment's notice is "rhyme time." Have students tell you what the main topics of recent classes have been. Write their responses on the board as they toss them out. Prompt any major misses with some hints after they seem to run out of ideas.

Next, have pairs of students around the room claim a topic. As each topic gets chosen, put a check next to it on the board. If there are an equal number of topics and groups, or if there are more topics than groups, you're good to go. If you run short of topics, either double up on one or pause to gather a few more topics. In their groups, have students write a four-lined rhyme that uses the topic somewhere in the first two lines, and any other topic in the final two. Follow with having the groups share what they've done.

Ideally, this yields some clever and funny items that prompt good review discussions. You can also ask the class to associate any unused terms with lines that the students wrote. If there isn't enough time for that, they can do so as an optional addition to the homework and see what happens. If no one adds anything, no worries. If someone comes up with something cool, all the better. That's good fodder for a college recommendation you might write later on why the student is self-directed with regard to creative applications of her or his work.

The ready-to-go activities above can be done with almost any age group in varying amounts of time. Figure out what students seem to like, and ask them for ideas on how to tweak the activities for future use.

You might also brainstorm some other types of ready-to-go activities in a staff meeting with colleagues. Not only can that help build a culture of using time well at a school, but it is probably time better spent than having someone read a list of announcements that could have been sent in an email.

Chapter 20

Take an Interest in Service Connections to Projects

"Can we put that video on our site?"

This question came from a director of a charity who wanted to use a student-created video that told the charity's story. The students had submitted the video to NextVista.org's annual Service via Video contest. (See a selection of those videos here: tinyurl.com/NV-service-finalists.)

Earlier, I mentioned the value of having an audience for student work. It's one thing to turn in work for a class. It's another for it to be appreciated by people outside the school. Students' ownership of learning and pride in their work reaches yet another level when that appreciation is part of a request that recognizes the professional value of the work. For the students who created this particular video, the charity director's request may have been the first time they realized they are capable of producing what a business wants and needs.

Opportunities and recognition like that can be a major boost for a student's creative confidence. But acquiring that kind of confidence requires putting themselves and their work in front of an audience first. It requires vulnerability. As Roni Habib, founder of EQ Schools, explains, "Vulnerable is real; not making mistakes is not."

Creative confidence can come when students see that what they produce offers real benefits for others. Each step further they push themselves opens up new possibilities for their own efforts. Even better, by going beyond the limited set of talents that the student already knows others appreciate, the student opens him- or herself up to criticism. And learning to look for what's useful in criticism means that vulnerability gives one the chance to become stronger.

Teachers face exactly the same set of challenges as they look at what they are willing to try in their lessons. The more they push themselves to try new things, the greater the number of tools at their disposal as they encounter new challenges. Embracing colleagues' or even students' ideas on what they've tried is the vulnerability that allows them to become stronger teachers and, arguably, stronger people.

This brings us back to the idea of service. Helping those who help others can build strengths and confidence about capabilities. The teacher can then use those experiences as stories to inspire other students.

Several years ago, students from a school in San Jose, California, created a video about an organization called Get on the Bus they submitted to NextVista.org. (You can watch it here: nextvista.org/get-on-the-bus.)

Students at the school gathered toys and food for goodie bags for the children who take the bus to visit a parent in prison. These children sometimes ride seven or eight hours to go to the prison for the once-a-year visit with the parent.

The students tell the video viewers what they learned from the experience, how they appreciate what they see as their more favorable situations, and how they are glad to be able to help the children in the program.

This is a story that can be used to remind the students that they have the strength, talents, and heart to help others.

In my almost thirty years as an educator, I have seen so many students let worries about what happens in their lives hold them back. I've also seen students excel when they choose to be vulnerable and step outside their own worlds long enough to help someone else. Sometimes that help comes in the form of creating a video that promotes a worthy cause. Sometimes it comes from setting up a fundraiser or toy drive, or from volunteering to serve in a soup kitchen or animal shelter.

If you aren't sure how to incorporate a service activity into what you do with your students, announce in a staff meeting that you are interested in working with one or more colleagues but need their ideas and contacts. The vulnerability of asking for help may create new connections and new professional confidence for you.

Chapter 21

Require Written Explanation on Their Plans for Improvement

See if this sounds familiar: Your students turn in essays or projects, and you spend an entire weekend painstakingly going over their work, writing up notes and advice to go with their grade. Monday, you hand everything back, giving them time to look over what you put together for them. A few students give the comments a cursory glance, but most look at the grade, compare grades with nearby students, and put (or throw) the papers away, giving somewhere between minimal and no attention to all you wrote.

Rather disheartening, that.

It might be expecting a little much to hope for students to react with something along the lines of, "My teacher put a lot of time into this; I'll make sure to learn from every comment!"

Such students are out there. There are also black swans in the world.

You know that if the students really worked with what you'd written, they might make some measurable improvements right away. So how do you help them do that?

One way is to require them to create their own digital or physical document outlining each of your comments, and explaining how they can incorporate that into an improved submission. This may sound like more work, and that's because it is.

"Why do that?" some would ask. "Just have them improve what they turned in before and submit the improved version."

You could easily require the explanation alongside an improved paper or project. But, requiring a written explanation of how the student is addressing concerns allows you to read what they are thinking. It also provides ample material for you to use as part of individual or parent meetings.

> Anytime you can get students to think in terms of doing a job well the first time, you're doing them a favor.

Aside from those benefits, setting the expectation for resubmission (with the accompanying explanation of how feedback is being addressed) may motivate students to turn in their best work the first time in order to avoid more work later. Anytime you can get students to think in terms of doing a job well the first time, you're doing them a favor.

One way to help them achieve that goal is to have students get meaningful feedback from other students before they turn in their work to you. I would suggest requiring that students get three meaningful pieces of feedback prior to submitting it and documenting how they used that feedback to better their work. This documentation could be turned in as a component of the final essay, project, etc. in the same way a student would add a bibliography to a research paper.

The operative term here is "meaningful." Comments like, "It's fine," aren't helpful. Instead, require that they get a suggestion, and that they write up their own ideas for choosing whether they followed or rejected the suggestion. Students don't need to debate the merits of the suggestions with the peers offering the advice, of course. Instead, they simply need to write down what the other person says, and then ask any clarifying questions before thanking them.

I can hear the objection now: "That's a lot of paper to keep up with." Perhaps, but not so much that a good paper clip or, better yet, digital collaboration tool couldn't resolve that issue. Remember, the most important issue is to ensure that students make progress via every assignment they do. Expanding the requirements for an essay or project to make it more meaningful may actually reduce the number of assignments/projects you give because the revised project is more thorough than one that has been quickly slapped together. If so, it's worth doing.

Chapter 22

Improve Grades and Understanding with a Pre-Final

I n theory, a final exam is an opportunity for the students to show just how much of the content they've mastered. In reality, students commonly experience some memory loss (a masterpiece of understatement, perhaps) throughout the term or school year. Without a certain amount of review to help solidify students' understanding (and jog their memory) of the key concepts, the final exam isn't an accurate reflection of the learning that has taken place.

To address this reality, I gave a "pre-final" two weeks before the formal finals week at the end of each semester. The pre-final was structured exactly as the final exam in terms of the sections, point values, and level of difficulty. The questions and challenges changed from one to the next, but the preparation required of the students was exactly the same.

"What?" you may exclaim. "You doubled your work with the biggest exam of the term? That sounds a bit masochistic to me."

It was more work to do a pre-final, but not double. And I believed it was worth the effort because what truly mattered was whether students had learned the content.

The idea of a really big test may seem like something that wouldn't merit a student's welcome, but many of my students actually appreciated the pre-final because it helped them get in gear to prepare for finals. Aside from helping them study for the final earlier than they would have without the pre-final, I offered a couple of other carrots.

First, to entice students to prepare well, I used the score on the pre-final to replace their most damaging two quiz/test scores from the semester, as long as this proved beneficial to their grade. My logic was that they may have needed a little longer to get some concepts down, and by showing that they had done so on the pre-final, I was happy to reward them in this way.

This requires some work with regard to one's math and grades. I used a fairly involved spreadsheet to take the percentage score from the pre-final, apply it to show the corresponding grades for comparison with earlier tests, and pick out what would be most helpful to the student.

For example, if a student got an 80 percent on the pre-final, and during a tough period earlier in the term had failed two 30-point quizzes with scores of 12 and 14, I would change both to 24 (80% of 30). That's like giving him or her an extra 22 points (the difference between the two scores of 24 and the previous scores), and it reflected mastery of the material, as long as I had done a good job constructing the exam.

This also gave me a good point of discussion with parents. Students who performed poorly early on would get something of a second chance, albeit at a time when they were being asked to work with the entire term's content. In other words, students really had to be on their game to take advantage of this offer.

Second, any student who achieved an "A" grade on the pre-final could opt out of the final exam. I would simply apply the grade from the pre-final to the final, and that would be that. Those students were welcome to use time in class for the last two weeks of the term to prepare for other exams. The opportunity to have one fewer final to study for was one of the favorite perks for my students.

For those who didn't get an "A", I would spend the last week before finals focusing on their challenges with the material, sometimes helped by students who had earned the right not to have to take the final exam.

Some teachers have asked me, "If students didn't have to take the final, why should they bother showing up to class?"

Given the structure of our school, it was important that students continue to attend, but I had no problem with this. Why? Because part of the deal for being exempt from the final exam was that they had to show up, on time, with something quiet to do. If they walked into the final exam period even a second late, they would be expected to take the final.

A student did show up a minute late once. I gave him a final to take. He was a little stunned that I'd been telling the truth the many times I'd reminded them they had to be on time, but he took the exam, and did well enough not to have his grade slip.

From then on, I could add when explaining the rules that it had happened that a student had shown up late for a final and I'd followed through with the promise that the student would have to take the test. Evidence that you're serious is a blessed thing.

To recap, there were three big reasons to study one's posterior off for the pre-final:

1. It was a big, whopping test all by itself worth a lot of points.

2. The percentage score earned could be used to replace two of the most damaging quiz/test scores from the semester.

3. Doing really well would mean not having to take the final exam, making the end of the term a notch less stressful.

Using a tool like the pre-final well required having a full description of the structure and logic of the test in the syllabus. I also made sure my principal was well aware of what I was doing and had given it his blessing.

The bottom line is that you should figure out what can help your students master the class content, discuss with colleagues and students what they think of it, and keep refining it as you go. The extra work may be easily worth it when it clearly benefits your students.

Discussion Items for
AREA 2: Assignments and Assessments

In your team meetings or brainstorming sessions with colleagues, use the following questions to explore possibilities for strengthening the effectiveness of assignments and assessments. As you come up with more questions like these that prove useful, please share them at tinyurl.com/MYTSS-suggestions.

1. Do you give students options with some of their assignments? If so, what do they seem to choose to do, and why? If not, is there an upcoming assignment which would be good for offering options?

2. How do you get students to give you more interesting work? Have you asked them to make what they do fascinating? If so, how did it go? If not, would you try it for an upcoming assignment?

3. Which assignments or projects best show the range of things students learn in your class? How can you give them examples of both less and more successful student work?

4. What characteristics of extra-credit work allow it to genuinely enhance their learning?

5. What are topics that students find challenging every year? Can you have students try creating videos or other resources that address those topics in different ways? Would time spent making such videos be productive for them, as well?

6. What is the least valuable assignment you give? Should you keep it? If so, how can you make it more valuable for their learning?

7. Have you created a quick activity which proved both engaging for students and effective for their learning? What are the coolest ready-to-go activities you've seen used?

8. What social/community causes are most important to you, and how might they relate to what you teach? How can you get students' interests in helping the community to be part of your class?

9. What are the most effective and/or novel ways you've seen students work with the feedback they receive?

10. At what point each school year do students most effectively show what they have learned? If that moment is an exam, how do you keep it from being one for which they cram, take the test, and forget the material?

Area 3

Delivery

Chapter 23

Start Class with Something Unpredictable

et's say that you are about to begin a science unit on primates. You could begin by announcing you're about to start teaching them about primates. It's a true statement, but it doesn't provide much fodder for sparking curiosity.

Alternatively, you could show a short video about Jane Goodall, the scientist who spent more than five decades studying chimpanzees in Tanzania. That would provide visuals which could allow students to connect what you teach to what they've seen, which makes for a good strategy. And if you stop the video several times to ask students what they think they're seeing, it becomes an interactive experience in which they try to associate what they see and hear with what they may already know about Goodall, chimps, Africa, or something else.

Another approach to piquing interest for your primate study is to start class with this quote:

"The least I can do is speak out for those who cannot speak for themselves."

Don't let them know it's from Goodall. Instead, ask them to find who said this, how that person is known, and what questions it may raise for what they might learn next.

What they discover probably won't change the meat-and-potatoes information you provide as they learn about primates, but it could provide some early ideas about what they might explore further, if you give them that opportunity. And they may even recall that quote later in the year during a discussion about compassion, or government, or choosing a life of service.

Both the video and the quote have a specific advantage for getting the unit going: The students aren't likely to see the activity of watching a story or researching a quote as a predictable piece of day-to-day schooling. It's engaging. It makes them want to know more. And that's the point. Getting each class or portion of your day off to an effective start helps your students see your classroom or learning space as a place where they expect more of themselves.

Start your class each day by inviting interaction and sparking curiosity.

Many of the best starters for class focus on questions requiring a little research and imagination, but too often, teachers start their lessons in rather uninspiring ways: "Alright class, let's settle down. We have some important stuff to cover today."

What? Was the stuff covered yesterday not important? Let's hope that's not what was meant!

Even worse, the teacher may start class with that line every day, which means it has lost any value as a differentiating description. Not to mention that "settle down" fails to inspire enthusiasm. Does "settle down" mean that the teacher isn't interested in getting participation in what's about to happen? The student may interpret that as a message to get passive and compliant right away, suggesting that nothing actively interesting is on the way, or that being in the class is more about the teacher's control than it is about their learning. Students who get the message to quiet down daily may get so quiet that they aren't interested in speaking up when the teacher does want to have a discussion.

Start your class each day by inviting interaction and sparking curiosity. Be intentional about engaging kids in the process of learning—a process that should be all about their seeing new possibilities in what you teach.

Chapter 24

Using Quiet to Your and Their Advantage

Constantly telling students to "settle down" before your lessons sends the message that the learning is going to be passive (aka boring). That isn't to say, however, that calling for a time of quiet can't be a good move for starting class.

My friend Roni Habib is one of those reflective, interesting, and funny teachers who is a joy to spend time with. He tells a story of starting a high school economics class with a bit of a departure from his standard pattern, telling the students something like this:

"Guys, I'd like to try something a little different today. I'm not sure it'll be something useful or interesting for you, and if you don't like it, then no worries, we won't try it again. I'd like to ask you to spend the next sixty seconds completely silent. Try not to think about the class, or anything else, if possible. Just concentrate on your breathing."

They gave it a shot, and he was ready for them to finish by bursting into laughter or playfully accusing him of a seriously crystal-rubbing-esque approach to his teaching. Still, he asked them what they thought of it.

Turns out they loved it.

These students go and go and go all day, constantly being reminded of what they need to get done soon, moving directly from one class and activity to another, and drowning in a sea of digital and face-to-face messages of all sorts. The chance just to be calm was something that they welcomed.

Roni noticed better focus and more productive engagement in learning on days when they started with a little quiet. Perhaps more powerful was the connection the students began to feel to this teacher who understood that they are people who need a moment just to breathe.

The opportunity to take a moment to step away from the what-needs-to-be-done-next rat race and just breathe isn't valuable only for the students, of course. Many teachers find that their time before school is all hurry-to-get-ready with no time to think creatively about what students may need. Taking a moment just to breathe, meditate, pray, or simply be quiet may allow you to take a major step in a positive direction, personally and professionally.

Roni's work with topics such as mindfulness, creative confidence, and emotional intelligence led him to start an organization called EQ Schools (EQSchools.com), which runs workshops to help participants, among other things, feel happier and collaborate with others more effectively.

It may sound a bit New Age-y, but if it works to help students learn more effectively and teachers find greater satisfaction with their work, I, for one, am all for it.

Chapter 25

Review Well by Not Saying Too Much

One standby for starting class is the teacher announcing that she or he would review what was covered in the last class, spend several minutes doing so, and then move into the day's lesson. Technically, it's a perfectly reasonable thing to do. In terms of educationally productive intrigue, it's as barren as a sand dune.

Yes, recapping what was covered in the last class may be important for tying it to what you are about to cover, but the question is whether you start by being the one who takes the active role in getting it on your students' radars.

Your spending time at the beginning of class repeating what you covered the day before sends two problematic messages.

First, it lessens the importance of keeping oneself focused during the current lesson. It'll be covered again at the beginning of the next class, after all.

Second, the implicit message to the class is that the work of the review is not on their shoulders, as the teacher has made it clear he or she will handle it. That is to say that the student is not asked to do anything other than listen. That may make sense at a symphony, but makes less sense if one's goal is for the students to develop a command of the content as quickly as possible.

A favorite technique for me is to start with an image—any image that won't get me fired—and ask the students to talk with each other about how that image relates to what was covered in the last class.

Consider this photograph I took on a weekend trip with my wife:

Half Moon Bay Tree at Sunrise by Rushton Hurley (CC by 4.0)
instagram.com/p/BMuC20yFGEH

Is it a nice picture? Yes. Do I know how it may relate to whatever I last covered? Nope.

I don't need to know. If the answer were obvious to me, it would be obvious to the students, as well, and if my tone weren't carefully crafted, I'd be giving them the message that I don't ask interesting questions of them. Not a good message, that.

If there's no clear connection, though, what students come up with would require some creative reaching, and in doing that, they would explore the ideas at a notably more interesting level than if I simply asked if they recalled what we covered.

That brings up the point that some would make, which is this: "All fine and good, but the issue is they don't remember what we covered, so I have to tell them! *Harumph.*"

While I appreciate a well-timed *harumph*, this is not one of those times.

I'd contend that students often have trouble remembering precisely because they expect that the teacher will have done the remembering for them by starting class with a passive review.

By asking them to talk to each other and relate what was covered to the image, they may well start by trying to recall what it was that did constitute the last lesson. Talking through that and thinking about components that may relate to the image, especially if they've learned to have a little fun when doing so, is a much more active way to get them to prepare for the day's new content.

Chapter 26

Use a Noisemaker (Not Your Voice) to Capture Attention

Do you have a cowbell? If not, there's something you need.

More cowbell.

It doesn't have to be an actual cowbell, but you do need something that can make a loud noise when you need to capture your class' attention.

Kids get loud from time to time. (If that statement doesn't apply to your classroom, I suspect you are either a wildly successful yoga teacher, or your students aren't learning as much in your class as would be ideal.)

Active learning typically involves an exchange of ideas, some trial and error, and/or plenty of encouragement the group gives to whichever member of the team is trying something at the moment. Silent, these things tend not to be, and that's a good thing! But, from time to time, enthusiasm about the task at hand or discussions that start up after they've completed (or lost focus on) a task will reach a volume that requires an immediate refocusing on you.

What I hope you will never do, barring a life-threatening situation, is yell to recapture students' attention. When the one adult in the room raises her or his voice, it suggests that person is losing control over the environment. It's an act that can make the students feel awkward, tense, or nervous for all sorts of reasons. Perhaps most important among those reasons is that, for some students, yelling is an indication that things are about to take a turn for the worse because that's what happens in their homes when an adult starts to yell. Many kids in abusive families learn to head for cover when someone yells, and for obvious reasons, you don't want to call those images to mind for them in your classroom.

So, instead of raising your voice, create a sudden noise. The ring of a cowbell, though loud, is completely nonthreatening and will quickly bring all eyes back to you. Be ready with a smile and a calm voice, and share a thought along these lines: "Yes, and that brings us to the next point I want to make…."

> ## Most students quite like knowing someone in the room who is not their age is in charge.

No nagging, no exasperation. Let your voice and message carry the thought that all is okay, and that you're moving forward. Most students quite like knowing someone in the room who is not their age is in charge.

As a native Texan, being able to ring a cowbell at a rather stunning volume comes quite naturally. Early in my teaching, I managed to master the calm smile while shaking the windows with the power of my cowbell. Good times.

Using that noisy metallic beast was something I only had to do for a few weeks. After that, if the class was going in a direction I thought was problematic, all I had to do was pick up that wonderful little gem. The students close by would immediately shush the others while throwing their hands over their ears in anticipation of the daunting decibels I could produce.

Students who engage in the bad karma of trying to get under your skin are likely ones who most need to know that an adult can greet such dishonorable decisions with measured calm. Hearing you raise your voice may be one of the easiest ways for them to know when they've succeeded in taking control from you. Don't give them that satisfaction. Rattle that cowbell instead, keep calm, and carry on with class.

Chapter 27

Know the Two-Minute Summary

If you ask your students at the end of class today to tell you the most important points from the lesson that just ended, would they be able to answer accurately?

More to the point, if a student who was absent asked you what the most important point from yesterday's lesson was, would you be able to summarize it helpfully?

I suspect that in terms of helpful summaries, there are three groups of teachers.

The first group comprises those teachers who can quickly and clearly relate the key pieces of the previous lesson. The larger set of connections and the activities designed to help students fully appreciate the ideas will be let go, but the summary will be a succinct framework for thinking about where the class was and where it is going.

The second group consists of those who can identify the main points, but don't succinctly provide a way of thinking about what is more and what is less important among them. The poor student who was absent will get the answer to his question, but will walk away not knowing how to connect those key points to what the class will learn next.

The third group includes those who have trouble describing the previous class without touching on every last thing covered. In a hurry to have mentioned everything, they cover the ideas at a speed which leaves the student feeling as if he just drank from a fire hose. That kind of overwhelming, all-encompassing "summary" can, obviously, be intimidating for the average student.

The teachers' intentions are good in all three groups. They want the student who missed class to get caught up as quickly as possible. It's true that a few people have a knack for succinct, relevant summations, but what is more likely is that those in the first group have simply taken time to do a bit of preparation.

For every lesson you teach, it is a worthwhile practice to articulate the main points in a two-minute summary. Exactly how long it takes to provide a proper summary will change with the topic and focus of the students, but there are advantages in having rehearsed it before a student asks, "What did we do yesterday?"

Clearly, being able to offer a two-minute summary will be useful in helping someone who missed class, but that isn't the only benefit. If, as you plan your lesson, you can articulate the main ideas students should know when they walk out of the room, your activities are likely to be more focused on ensuring that students have a confident command of what you covered.

And if you do this for every class, connecting components of each topic to the main points of previous lessons should be all the easier.

So think back to your last lesson. Can you clearly summarize the main pieces in about two minutes? If not, you may want to reorganize your approach to the next lesson.

Chapter 28

Give Credit Where Credit Is Due

Being educated is, in part, being able to identify what is one's own, and what comes from someone else. Ideally, we're helping students identify and build upon what they hear and read.

This is true for even the youngest ones. Imagine something like this: "Chris said I can't play on the seesaw, but I think the seesaw is for everyone." A good discussion can follow from the ideas, rather than the teacher simply being a referee between two students at odds over playground equipment.

When exploring writing, we ask students to identify sources, then provide thoughts on the material. As they get older, they learn about bibliographies and hopefully how to determine the value of the sources. And we obviously don't want them taking what others have written and suggesting it is their own work.

But do students understand the need to cite sources and avoid plagiarism? In the Digital Age, when it's so easy to find all sorts of writing online, I would argue that many students don't fully understand this basic piece of education. They need us to help them know what represents appropriate use of others' ideas and work.

So what do we model for them? Hopefully we are fairly good about this with text, but one way in which we commonly fail to model appropriate use is in the realm of digital media. It is the rare teacher creating slides for a presentation who will cite an image found online, and an even rarer one who will go the extra step of finding and citing an image that is legally usable beyond the classroom. If even one student in the class sees you ignore rules for citing sources, the word will get around quickly that you aren't serious about it when asking them to do the same.

A savvy teacher might note that in the United States and some other countries, teachers may use copyrighted content in the classroom specifically for educational purposes. However, in an age in which we increasingly take advantage of the opportunity to share things students create with a large audience online (international partner schools, science fairs, media festivals, etc.), we must recognize that the Fair Use provisions that protect the use of copyrighted content in the classroom do not apply in these broader (and potentially more intellectually dynamic) environments.

> We should model the practice of providing citations for everything, even when it is our own work

If you aren't already familiar with the term "Creative Commons," this is a good one to learn and use with your students. Creative Commons is a form of copyright in which the person who wrote the text, took the picture, played the music, etc., gives anyone permission to use it for free, as long as the source is cited. There are some variations on this requirement, and exploring it is beyond the scope of this book. I would encourage you to learn much more about it at CreativeCommons.org.

What this licensing system provides, though, is much greater than simply keeping you and your students on the right side of legal. It means that there is an almost endless supply of music, images, footage, and writings we can access for free by following the proper rules.

As part of a larger push for what is sometimes called "the sharing economy," Creative Commons-licensed content has the potential to level several of the academic playing fields on which our students learn. For example, students can build presentations using actual historical images (like the one below) without needing their school to be close to a major museum or to have expensive resource libraries.

Roman Ruins, Palmyra, Syria
by Le Grand Portage from Wikimedia Commons (CC by 2.0)
commons.wikimedia.org/wiki/File:Roman_ruins,_Palmyra,_Syria.jpg

We have explored several possibilities in this book for using images to enhance learning activities. Each time you do this in class, you can underscore this larger message about citing sources by providing the name of the image, the person or entity responsible for it, the site from which you got it, and (ideally) links and the Creative Commons license that applies.

There are times when we as teachers are not required by law to cite sources for material we use. However, for bolstering our students' understanding of what is and isn't appropriate with what we find online and elsewhere, we should model the practice of providing citations for everything, even when it is our own work.

Rodin Garden at Stanford
by Rushton Hurley from Flickr (CC by 2.0)
flickr.com/photos/rushtonh/32432861553

Chapter 29

Avoid Bad Questions

Teachers ask lots of questions. Good questions are those that get students thinking along creative lines, making connections for themselves, and, ideally, understanding that they're capable of thinking at higher levels than they knew.

The more good questions we ask, the better off our students will be. But questions that fall far short of "good" get asked far too often.

Asking ridiculously easy questions, for example, can do more harm than good—particularly when asking in such a way that suggests students don't know the answer. "You don't remember why this is important?" said in an annoyed tone will do little to create an atmosphere of intellectual intrigue.

Such a question can create an awkward environment for everyone and make it difficult to get things back on a productive track.

That isn't to say that easy questions won't be challenging for some in the room. The larger problem is that if you get a struggling student to work up enough confidence to offer an answer, and it turns out to be incorrect, then others may see that student as stupid for not knowing the answer to something simple. If you need to review simpler questions, it might be better to have them write down the answer to the question you just asked and then give them the correct answer, so that they can make sure they know where they are with the idea.

The more good questions we ask, the better off our students will be.

The truly pernicious questions, though, are the ones that seem to be perfectly natural for you to ask, but are actually making students feel less and less capable of handling what you're teaching.

One of those questions is this: "Who doesn't understand?" The intention may have been downright saintly. You want to know who is having trouble so you can help them get caught up. An honorable motive, this is. But if you ask, "Who doesn't understand?" and students simply stare at you, it's probably best not to assume everyone is on board with what you just taught.

More likely, the students believe that raising their hands will identify them to their peers as the dunces in the room. Given a choice between risking the stigma of being perceived by peers as dumb and missing the chance to let you know they're having difficulties, they'll likely choose the latter.

There are good tools for finding out where students are with content without having them convey their misunderstandings to the entire room. One way is through easy online survey tools (a simple Google Form, for example) that give you a quick breakdown of who is getting the ideas and who isn't, which is a good expression of formative assessment.

On a less technological level, you might have students hold up one of two index cards, one with a check mark on it and the other an "X," to let you know where they are. If everyone shows them to you and no one looks around, this can be a comfortably anonymous way to get feedback quickly.

Another really common and ineffective question is this one: "Who knows the right answer?"

This could be considered, in terms of intention, a nicer version of "Who doesn't understand?" It, too, does little to help most teachers know who is actually having issues.

When the students expect that raising a hand may result in being called on in front of others, there's plenty of risk, and minimal upside, to putting themselves in the position of being asked. Getting it wrong may be awkward, and it's probably better to let someone else take the risk, which leads us to what actually happens when teachers ask this question.

That is, when a teacher asks, "Who knows the right answer?", most of the room defers to the three or four students who always seem to get the right answer. That may be wonderfully validating for those three or four, but does little to push the rest of the class into taking an active role in learning.

None of this is to say that our job is to protect fragile egos by never focusing on misconceptions. Really good questions have everyone working on an idea, talking with each other to pull pieces together. Having students work together to develop their understanding also means that you can circulate and check with those struggling in a more inconspicuous way.

It is worth the reminder that when you do move around to help students, make sure to also stop and check in with students who aren't having problems, so that the act of stopping to talk with someone doesn't become associated with struggling.

Does all that make sense? If not, check in with me later—there's no need to raise your hand.

Chapter 30

Be Comfortable and Constructive with Your Lack of Omniscience

Every year in my beginning Japanese language classes, I devoted the first three days to introducing the fundamental syllables and how to read them. Many had clever mnemonic devices, which added to the fun. The syllable "nu," for example, looked a bit like two chopsticks and some noodles, and the "noo" of "noodles" was the sound for "nu."

Years into my career, I was taking the students through the flashcards and associated pictures, and got to the syllable "ho," which had some rather lame way of remembering it.

One student said, "You know, if you look at it sideways, it looks like it has an 'h' and an 'o' together." He was right, and I'd somehow never seen it before. I got downright jazzed by his observation, so much so that I'm sure my new students began wondering if I was even stranger than they'd heard.

I've never been one to hold back excitement for a cool idea, especially when it comes from a student. If you haven't already experienced a revelation moment in your class—with a student surprising you with an unexpected insight—let me assure you, it's great fun.

> ## I've never been one to hold back excitement for a cool idea, especially when it comes from a student.

Likewise, there will be days when students ask you a question to which they think you should know the answer, but you don't. You'll hear the proverbial crickets, and in that awkward moment a panicked voice in your head may chastise you: How horrible that they would catch you without some answer regarding what you teach! Teaching means you know everything about the topic, right?

Of course not.

Still, admitting that you don't know something can be disconcerting. Initially, you might feel embarrassed by showing a "weakness" in not having a comprehensive mastery of your subject. When the voice of panic starts to give you grief, remind yourself that the primary job in any classroom is learning. Modeling that you are not afraid to do what you ask of your students every day can be a powerful teaching tool with students at every grade level.

High school students, as many adults might observe, suffer from the misconception that they know everything, when, in reality, their lack of experience means that they are far more likely to be closer to the other end of the scale regarding most subjects. The characterization may not be completely fair, but there is value in teaching them that one of the key pieces of being a confident adult is having no trouble admitting what you don't know—and being willing to learn more.

Middle school students, awkward examples of quirky neediness that they are, tend to appreciate adults who show calm confidence. Given how much of their interaction with each other can involve substantial mood swings, instilling any sense that it's possible to be comfortable with what we can't do can be reassuring.

Elementary and younger students are often surprised when a teacher admits to being clueless about something. At such a moment, the opportunity is ripe for talking about how one might learn more about the idea—what kinds of questions to ask, how to look for answers, and how to discern which answers are best.

Encouraging students to be willing to search for answers is empowering, but it can be counterproductive to respond to every question by saying, "I don't know. Please look that up and report back to me tomorrow." It may not be constructive to convey that when they identify something you don't know, the result is more work for them.

Instead, give students room to work with you when you don't know something. They tend to like seeing someone pursue his or her curiosity. By thinking out loud as you explore the idea together, you may articulate connections that you've covered before, but that they hadn't fully mastered. The review may be welcome, particularly when it doesn't specify one or more learners as being behind.

And ask for their ideas. They may hit you with something that gets you downright jazzed.

Chapter 31

Be Prepared to Avoid Helping

Don't you feel great when you help a student work through a tough problem?

Sure you do. The look of thanks you get from the student is personally rewarding, and they may even be ready to move on to the next idea.

That said, try not to do that too much.

Lisa Highfill is a friend, a talented presenter, and a coauthor of *The HyperDoc Handbook* (tinyurl.com/y98vwane). She has presented around the United States on a variety of topics, including sessions on this idea of helping "too much."

As Lisa addresses the topic of "too much," she often shows a video with a mother duck leading her brood of ducklings up a step. Many of the ducklings have a rough go of it and need multiple attempts to fly high enough to join the successful group. After some time, there is only one duckling left who hasn't made the jump. The mother duck watches. She could easily plop down to help, but doesn't. Instead, she waits.

Failure after failure becomes harder and harder for us as the viewers to watch, but finally, the duckling makes it, and they head off in search of some duck-friendly spot.

The lesson for teachers is obvious: We tend to step in and help struggling students when given the opportunity because, quite simply, it feels good to be the hero. Go, us!

What the duckling learned, though, is that it can make that leap without help.

When our students achieve something that is difficult at first, their achievement provides solid evidence of capability. The strengthened confidence they develop will serve them well as they continue with the curriculum going forward.

So, although it feels good to swoop in and save the day, the strengthened confidence students experience when we watch and wait as they work out the problem on their own may well be a better way to "help" them win. Clearly, if you have to choose between the two, letting the student have the victory is the better choice.

As Lisa asks, "What do your actions show the learner about their ability to solve a problem?"

Waiting for a student's light-bulb moment is fairly easy when it's clear the student will overcome the current challenge. But what if you suspect the student will give up too soon? There are at least three steps you might take to help.

First, encourage without any guidance related to content. "I know you can do it," or, "You're close," or, "Have you tried thinking about it in a different way?" might give the student enough *umph* to try again and succeed. If this works, you can point out honestly that you didn't provide any new information, which provides evidence for the student as to his or her own capability.

Second, you can give partial information, working to say as little as possible in order to leave the student enough room to know that he or she can put the pieces together. Saying too much risks instilling the student with the belief that you'll need to be there for the next challenge. Although it may feel good to be needed, that's clearly not the purpose of your instruction.

Third, you can give the student a simpler problem to work with that may focus more directly on the concept that is proving to be the barrier to meeting the original challenge. This depends on the challenge being one that can be simplified, of course, as well as your being prepared to present the simpler problem if the need arises. When planning, it's always good to ask yourself what you'll do if a student can't seem to grasp what you're teaching.

There will be times when you may need to give the student the answer in order to keep things moving. When that happens, make time in the following day or two to get the student to give it a try again, so that he or she can overcome the challenge without your help.

If having to provide answers to keep things going happens often, you should consider the possibility that your lesson plans may need some tweaking. Consider the following questions:

- Do you give students enough time to be able to overcome common misconceptions?
- Do you provide challenging questions for those who succeed quickly, so those who are struggling have extra time to get the fundamental concepts down?
- Are any of the activities you've planned ones that could be discarded in order to give students more time to succeed and build their confidence?

Another question to ask yourself when students come to you for help is whether they do so because they think you'll provide the answer, thus allowing them to avoid going to the trouble of working hard on it themselves. It probably isn't news that many students develop some skills in this realm. If many are coming to you, it could be because they've figured out that you will enable such behavior.

I suspect you'd rather be known as someone who helped them learn to handle the challenges themselves.

If you have an aide or a teaching partner, make sure you are consistent with your approach. Any child lucky enough to have two parents at home will at some point test the possibility that a less-than-satisfactory response to a request made to one parent may be overturned by a more recent favorable response from the other. Be prepared to ask students what your co-teacher or assistant said or did in response to the same question.

Back to the duck.

Lisa and her colleagues Kelly Hilton and Sarah Landis share their HyperDocs ideas at HyperDocs.co to help teachers create activities that purposefully push students toward learning through active discovery. This kind of learning tends to be more effective than providing info that they are supposed to memorize. Having something to click on and explore, and then piecing together a larger story or picture of learning is interesting, and working together on well-designed challenges can help students help each other in constructive ways.

As you plan your learning activities, ask what might happen that could make you the mama duck from the story above. Do you know how to avoid helping too much?

Let's hope so. A student may need the boost in confidence enabled by your choice not to be the superhero.

Discussion Items for
Area 3: Delivery

In your team meetings or brainstorming sessions with colleagues, use the following questions to explore possibilities for strengthening your delivery of your lessons. As you come up with more questions like these that prove useful, please share them at tinyurl.com/MYTSS-suggestions.

1. How do you vary how you start class? What class starters have you done or seen that proved particularly interesting for students?

2. Would your students respond well to the idea of a minute of quiet? How do they find ways to bring a level of calm to their lives?

3. What works best for you for having students actively recall both recent and older material?

4. What kind of noisemaker (other than your voice) would best fit your personality for capturing students' attention?

5. When you ask students at the end of class to identify the most important elements of the lesson, under what conditions do they do a good job of it?

6. How do you make sure that students learn to cite their sources? Are there moments when you let them not bother doing so?

7. What questions do you regularly ask your students? How can you experiment with the questions to see whether you can improve upon the results you get?

8. Do you regularly ask students to describe other ways of thinking about what you've taught? If so, have there been moments when they surprised you with their insights?

9. How do you keep yourself from helping too much? Are there warning signs that let you know they are relying on you instead of themselves?

AREA 4

Collegiality and Professionalism

Chapter 32

Brainstorm with Colleagues

solation is the cancer of the educational system.

Thankfully, today, there's a cure.

When I first started mentoring teachers, the Internet was just coming into the public's consciousness. It seemed the vast majority of teachers in the American system, who were hired on the thought that they might just be able to do the job, were tossed into the deep end of that pool that is the classroom with the encouragement to swim.

If you were lucky, then there were people stationed at or visiting the school who regularly sat down with you to talk about approaches you were using. Perhaps such folks would share ideas with you about managing class and how not to get seriously depressed about the weight you felt was on your shoulders.

If you weren't so lucky, your first year was likely one of the toughest of your life.

The belief prevailed that, having been hired, it was somehow an epic failure to reveal that you didn't know how to deal with circumstances you may never have been prepared to encounter. Perhaps you even got the impression from some colleagues that the whole sink-or-swim thing was a hazing ritual that you either survived professionally—or didn't.

I remember beginning teachers breaking down into tears out of a sense of failure—of not being able to do what their students needed—despite how desperately they wanted these students to succeed.

Schools in my area of California have become much better at helping new teachers identify options for dealing with challenges. In a school that is a professionally and personally healthy place for teachers, folks take time to sit down with colleagues to toss ideas at each other, whether leadership provides identified time for this or not. Sometimes states take a hand in creating opportunities for mentorship. California, for example, requires new teachers to participate in what's commonly called Induction (formerly known as BTSA, or the Beginning Teacher Support and Assessment Program). The program gets a certain amount of eye-rolling from young teachers who see it as one more thing they have to do. Nonetheless, it provides teachers with regular time to connect and learn with others who are in the same place, professionally speaking.

I find it genuinely enjoyable to listen to people in this field talk about moments when they've stumbled onto something that worked really well. Some of my favorite moments involved sitting with colleagues and trying to figure out crazy approaches to using some tool or idea in our teaching.

If learning alongside others appeals to you, then go to a colleague and ask when they might have some time to do a little brainstorming. You'll likely get one of two responses.

One is from those who will claim, politely or less so, they don't have time for such things. My take? That's cover for not wanting to show that they aren't doing anything creative in class, and believe that others won't know if they just keep to themselves. Well, others do know, and now you do, too. No need to waste your time with that person.

The other and, I hope, more likely response is that they'd be glad to sit down with you. The chances are good that they know that such time is well spent. These people also know they can learn something from listening to how you see the world, however different your tallied years of teaching experience may be.

One very good way of dealing with worries about failure is to get excited about possibilities you want to try. Brainstorming is not just good for you professionally. It's good for you personally, too.

Chapter 33
Attend Gatherings

"What? All day Saturday? No way, that's my time off!"

And all you did was suggest attending an Edcamp. If the term "Edcamp" is new to you, you should know that it involves no tents or sleeping on the ground, although I'd contend those are good things to use and do every so often.

An Edcamp (Edcamp.org) is sometimes referred to as an "unconference" because the sessions aren't planned ahead of time. Like a more formal conference, it's a gathering of professionals interested in discussing ideas and learning new approaches to their work. Unlike more formal conferences, these events are normally free of any registration cost.

The difference between Edcamps and other conferences becomes pretty clear once you arrive at one of these shindigs. It's a laid-back event. (Anyone who shows up formally dressed is either new or doesn't own blue jeans; either way, they're still welcomed.) Organizers check you in and let you know that if there's a discussion you want to have, you are welcome to describe it on one of the post-it notes they provide and then add it to the board with the other post-it notes.

"I want to talk about working with just-arrived students who don't speak English."

"Would love to talk about video projects related to student community service."

"Looking for ideas for engaging colleagues who said 'No way!' to attending an Edcamp."

People add whatever has been on their minds and hearts, and after some amount of time, the organizers will take the suggestions and spread them across an agenda for the day. They combine items that seem to cover similar ground and try to keep topics that look like they'll be a big draw from conflicting on the schedule.

After an initial gathering which includes having the layout explained (giving time to the organizers to get the topics distributed among the time slots and rooms available), folks will see—on a big board, an online chart, or both—what session topics are available. Then everyone troops off to the rooms of their choice.

In the room, the person whose suggestion ended up as the topic will explain what he or she had in mind, and the participants can then begin sharing ideas. If it isn't what you wanted, you are welcome to leave and join another conversation; no one will take offense. The conversation may quickly move in a totally different direction. That's okay, too.

An amazing amount of good brainstorming happens at Edcamps. And it's that brainstorming that holds the appeal. Attendees are both serious about the ideas, and also plenty ready to share laughs about the work we all do. One reason Edcamps are popular is that they are a refreshing alternative to a professionally dysfunctional environment. For those attending an Edcamp from schools where strong brainstorming happens easily and productively, the ideas are all the more easily shared with folks once you get back to work the next week.

For those from a school where collegial brainstorming is rare at best, these events can be invigorating departures from their norm.

We all need time to get away from our work, and the colleague who refused your suggestion to attend may well need to just get away from all his or her professional duties for the weekend. That's fair enough. But getting together with colleagues from other schools, and especially from other kinds of schools (traditional public, charter, religious, or independent), can be great for getting your own juices flowing.

In addition to Edcamps, there are many other kinds of gatherings that can reenergize you. Traditional conferences can be excellent opportunities to see what others are doing, learn about new products that are available, and hear speakers who have inspiring messages.

If you prefer the informal setting, but don't want to give up an entire day, you might try to find out if there are coffeeEDU gatherings (CoffeeEDU.org) nearby. These tend to be one-hour events, with people taking time to share ideas over a little caffeine. Decaf folks are welcome, too. These events happen when someone puts the idea of getting together on social media and identifies a place and time. Whoever shows up, shows up. Even if the ideas aren't so great, you may feel the time was well spent if your coffee was tasty.

If you can't find a coffeeEDU event nearby, try hosting one yourself. The number of people who show up isn't important. What is important is having an outlet to share ideas and connect with other teachers. The ideas that percolate may be exactly what you need to bring life to an upcoming unit, find something that saves you lots of time, or help you connect with a student who's been causing problems in class.

Chapter 34

Don't Reinvent
the Wheel

Time (or lack thereof) may well be a teacher's greatest source of stress.

Will I be able to cover everything I am supposed to cover?

Am I packing enough in so that they'll be ready for this or that test?

Do I have a lesson plan ready for tomorrow?

Trying to keep up with curricular demands, while trying to pay attention to the needs of all your students, while trying to respond to requests for information from the school or district, while trying to communicate effectively and regularly with parents, while trying to do all this and stay sane—it's not an easy job.

One way to reach maximum stress with time is to look at what needs to be created or designed for your class, and decide to do all the needed work on your own. One way to reduce stress is to stop trying to do it all.

Are there clever activities, well-organized presentations, and helpful videos out there available for you to use in your class? Yes! And if you decide to ignore this rather helpful component of the information society, that's your (bad) decision.

Before you design a lesson from scratch, consider what resources are already available. Simply doing a web search for lesson plans for your topic and level (elementary fractions lesson plans, or middle school rock cycle lesson plans, or high school Spanish subjunctive verbs lesson plans, etc.) can yield plenty of ideas. Not everything you find will be good, but plenty of even what's weak is probably adaptable in some way that could help your students.

> # Before you design a lesson from scratch, consider what resources are already available.

Incorporating ideas from other teachers into your lessons also provides an opportunity, as encouraged earlier, to model citing your sources. If you find that a teacher has posted a cool lesson plan on the life cycle of a butterfly at Curriki.org, for example, then tell the students that Teacher X from School Y in Place Z created something you adapted for the day's class. You can even have the class give that person a hand to emphasize the coolness of sharing good ideas with others.

While I would hope it doesn't need to be said, never take someone else's work and pretend it's your own. That's a move that could get you fired. As you'd expect, suggesting through one's actions that it's okay to lie about what you do is frowned upon.

But what if what makes you frown is the poor quality of something you find online? Well, bad material may be the basis for a good activity. "Students, I'll show you a video on the food pyramid posted by HazardKiddo33 on YouTube. So you know, it's pretty bad. In your groups, your job is to come up with at least five reasons why. Style points for suggestions that no other groups think of."

A big reason for using what is freely available online is that it saves you time. It isn't the only reason, though. Consider the value of looking at how others approach the lessons you teach. You might find that a teacher in Toronto has a really clever way of approaching something you've had difficulty teaching for years. You may take something a teacher in Houston created, adapt it in some interesting way, and then share what you did with that teacher, which could save that person the time of improving it as they prepare the activity for future classes.

The old saying goes this way: "Many hands make light work." Teachers all over the world are creating and posting and borrowing and adapting all sorts of materials. Joining in on all these fronts makes you a globally creative colleague with a little more time and a lot less stress.

Chapter 35
Use Student-Audience Videos for Professional Development

A teen boy mostly covered in aluminum foil leaps in front of a whiteboard.

"Hey friends! Do you know what time it is?"

From the area that is clearly behind the camera, a chorus of students shouts, "What time is it?"

A second teen, also copiously covered in foil, leaps into the picture. "It's FOIL time!"

The off-screen chorus cheers.

They go on to describe the FOIL method of multiplying binomials, with more moments of silliness that somehow don't get in the way of the message.

If you need to be reminded of how something works, wouldn't you rather see it in a way that makes you smile? And if you need to see the process lots of times, it's pretty nice to have a video, which allows you to restart again and again.

The video described above, "FOIL Time" (nextvista.org/foil-time), was a finalist in one of my nonprofit's earliest contests. It has been seen hundreds of times on NextVista.org. In addition to being a concise reminder of an algebraic concept, the video could be something you use with colleagues to discuss questions like the following:

- Is this a video that would help a struggling student?

- Would it be better if it addressed something commonly misunderstood in the lesson? Would the misconception be better as the focus of its own video?

- What are other ways a teacher (or students) might explain the idea?

- Can we have students in different classes make videos about several concepts in order to try and gather a library of review items for everyone? If so, should we get them posted at NextVista.org? (A toothy smile with a visible sparkle and *ping!* sound goes here.)

Having this kind of discussion with colleagues can generate some strong insights on what works well for students, how to overcome misconceptions, and how to implement projects that have students creating materials others can use to review.

Let's work with another example.

The video fades in from black, with a boy about nine years old dressed in detective clothing sitting by a desk with his feet propped up. A phone rings, and he leaps up to answer it.

"Hello! What? A vocabulary mystery? I'm on my way!"

He leaps from view, letting the receiver fall to the floor.

The scene changes, and three frustrated students are grappling with the word "vacant," which they've encountered in a sentence.

Our intrepid detective then helps various groups of students by describing vocabulary discovery strategies (breaking down words, looking for context clues, using pictures, and continuing to read).

The video ends with credits rolling and the students singing a song about how to figure out vocabulary to the tune of "Do You Know the Muffin Man?"

Cute? Certainly.

Was the "Vocabulary Mystery" video (nextvista.org/vocabulary-mystery) time-consuming to make? Probably so. But are the students who appeared in the video more likely to remember the content than if it had been covered in class in more traditional ways? When I have asked this question to teachers at talks I've given, most respond with an emphatic "Yes!"

What if the students don't remember the strategies? Well, they have a video they can go back to and watch, don't they? (Another sparkling *ping!* smile goes here.)

Short videos are a nice point of departure for a discussion of what works for learning. Sometimes you'll want videos with content that matches what you and your colleagues teach, but videos targeted at very different grade levels can also yield ideas for all kinds of approaches to projects and activities. If you're looking for ready-made student videos to use for discussion prompts or ideas in your staff meetings, look over this online doc with sets of student-created videos (tinyurl.com/NV-video-sets), or the collection of Next Vista contest finalists (nextvista.org/tag/finalist). Each video is limited to ninety seconds (with up to another sixty seconds for credits).

Does a short student video sound like a good addition to your grade-level or departmental meeting? You might be surprised at how many creative ideas a curmudgeonly colleague can come up with, given the opportunity.

Chapter 36

Question What We Have Done for Years

People who question the status quo are sometimes accused of wanting change "for the sake of change." As one who regularly puts too much onto his plate and in the interest of not adding anything unnecessary to my task list, I'm in favor of avoiding change for the sake of change.

That said, it makes no sense to avoid change simply to maintain the status quo.

Some of the things we do need to be improved upon, and some need to be eliminated altogether. Our job is to figure out what to stop doing, what to work on, and when to make the necessary changes based on our priorities.

When colleagues can get together and talk about common (and comfortable) practices with a critical eye, it's a sign that they want to improve not only their own practice, but also the larger organization— and perhaps even the entire field of education.

I recently got into a conversation with colleagues at a high school I visit regularly about the idea of a student writing one paper and turning it in to fulfill assignments in two different classes. The parameters and associated topics got very interesting, very quickly.

One teacher mentioned that this is plagiarism. As we explored the idea, it initially seemed strange to suggest that the term "plagiarism" fit in this situation since the work is by the student who is submitting it. Still, part of plagiarism is misrepresenting one's work, which could be the case in this example.

Another teacher suggested that a student would need to cite his or her work if referencing something done before. That certainly falls in line with modeling proper approaches to building on previous ideas.

A third teacher questioned whether it would even be possible to turn in an essay for a different assignment if the teacher had been properly specific about what was being required in the assignment. Clarity of purpose and detailed rubrics would address the issue of a paper that didn't fit, and the question would then center on how the student was representing the work.

Of course, it could be possible to have an assignment in which students are asked to take an essay they had done for a past class, and write an accompanying paper about how its content relates to topics being covered in the current class. Ideally, this might allow a student to take the learning that went into the first assignment and build on it in some interesting way. That raised the question of which has more value: two independent papers started from scratch, or one paper explored in more detail and along new lines.

An administrator looking at the idea pointed out that one approach to having students do work for multiple classes is to have teachers coordinate the assignments, and this school offers summer curriculum grants to teachers to plan such things. That's a cool, smart solution. In fact, as this school is working on the possibility of having a capstone project for students wanting to push themselves intellectually, thinking about this idea of drawing on work from multiple courses has proven useful.

Why is all of this interesting? In part, it's because there's something in our experience that suggests to us that any given assignment requires work started from scratch. However, if what's important is what the child learns, then the starting from scratch part seems less important.

> The more we take time to discuss with colleagues why we do what we do, the better what we do will become.

It should be noted that in graduate school and perhaps undergraduate study as well, there is the possibility that any given thing one writes could be published, and typically a publisher's expectation is that what they are putting out hasn't been published before. For younger students, though, we're training them to write in various ways, as opposed to expecting them to seek a publisher for the assignment they give us.

This dilemma of papers and self-plagiarism is only one example of any number of questions we could explore related to our underlying assumptions about the work we ask of our students. Not everyone is initially comfortable with questioning past practices, but the more we take time to discuss with colleagues why we do what we do, the better what we do will become.

Chapter 37

Avoid the Rancid Quagmire of Mediocrity

"**H**ey, Mr. Hurley! 'Avoid the rancid quagmire of mediocrity!'"

The speaker was a former student I hadn't seen in more than a decade. He was quoting me with a line I used from time to time to encourage my classes not to give in to the desire to simply check off boxes and, instead, to embrace the opportunity to explore fascinating details in what they were learning. I'd somehow got out of the habit of saying it, so hearing it quoted by a former student was a delightful surprise that connected me to a piece of my past that I was glad to encounter anew. That is, it's fun to remember the moments that added bits of interest and depth to the classes—and to know that those moments meant something to my students as well.

Not so much fun, though, is the mediocrity that we run into all the time. It could be a business where the person behind the counter shows little or no interest in treating you as a valued customer. It could be a contractor who is clearly not focusing on the details of something you are paying to have done. It could be a government office where the person behind the counter makes you wait so as to finish up a gossip session with a colleague.

You see mediocrity in students' work, as well. Any time the student's goal is something other than to do well on the task (just hand it in, guess and don't worry about it, get back to talking with a friend, etc.), that student moves another notch behind where she or he could be. The potential you know exists within that child dwindles day by day, an observation that is made all the more disheartening with the knowledge that the smallest amount of additional effort could start something powerful.

Mediocrity is a pattern into which a student can fall quite easily and, soon enough, the effort needed is not just to do the assignment, but to break the habit of not getting started.

Students aren't the only ones in schools who deal with these poor habits, either.

Disappointed and tired teachers slow down, calmly accepting that students will fail, and use that resignation as justification for not putting more into their teaching. Some will become very good at explaining why things colleagues want to try can't happen (which wouldn't be an issue if they were also bringing alternatives to the table, but they don't). Some will even begin to put whatever energy they have into blocking the efforts of others out of fear that another's success will highlight their own lack of effort.

While at a conference several years ago, the session leader challenged those of us in the audience to come up with ideas related to whatever she was presenting. I remember listening to one person at my table toss out an interesting thought, and then watching in dismay as another teacher launched into a litany of exasperated complaints about her students. For every idea we offered, she used another complaint or disparaging remark to shoot it down.

"All they want to do is go smoke their pot," she finally summed up, with a certain satisfaction at having thoroughly dampened the enthusiasm of almost everyone else at the table.

Ah, there but for the grace of God go I, I thought.

It is very easy to give up on a child, and I said so to this discouraging person at our table.

As I see it, it's a dangerous step to assume the lack of interest of a few students applies to everyone in the room. And deciding that students don't want to be in your classroom is a surefire way to make that come true. We don't need to tell our students what we believe about them. They'll know from our tone, our facial expressions, our positive encouragement (or lack of it), and our willingness or unwillingness to try anything to make a difference.

This isn't at all to say that those having trouble teaching are doomed to be forever mired in the counterproductive horror described above. Plenty of teachers want to do better and are willing to try whatever seems hopeful. Some simply need access to colleagues who will help them.

You may be the encouragement another teacher needs, and that doesn't require you to be a veteran. As a new teacher, you might be determined to let your good mood outlast the whining of a colleague trapped in negativity. It may take many conversations, and perhaps many years, to get through to someone who has given in to cynicism. Once a turning point happens, though (like the students you've been working with to get to believe in themselves for weeks or months), it's a pretty powerful moment.

There are all kinds of messages we give in our teaching. The little things we say and do—positive and negative—may stick in our students' or our colleagues' heads for a long, long time.

So, hey, avoid the rancid quagmire of mediocrity!

Chapter 38

Understand the Knife Edge of Comfort

Are you comfortable?

Comfortable can mean all sorts of things. If you have food to eat, a place to sleep, and clean clothes to wear, that represents one kind of comfort. We should remember that not all our students have these necessities.

If you have people who love you and whom you love, that's a level of comfort. Not all our students have this in their lives, either. We should note that some students have this, but don't know it, which is a different challenge.

Having a job working in a school and knowing that what you do each day can be meaningful to others can bring a sense of comfort. Lots of the other adults we encounter every day would not say this about their jobs, and many of them wish that they had made different choices along the paths of their lives.

A certain amount of comfort is necessary. Comfort can free us from pressing needs in order to be creative. Too much comfort, however, gears us down past neutral to a mediocre lack of momentum. Experiencing discomfort pushes us to expect and look for more or better ways to live and work. This truth applies especially well to the way we go about teaching.

I would venture to say that none of the very best teachers I have met are comfortable. Having their basic physical and emotional needs already met, they feel a sense of freedom, but they also have an edge to them; they know there is always room for improvement and are constantly interested in finding something new that might inspire a student. They have learned to leverage the interesting dynamic that exists between comfort and the excitement that comes from innovation, understanding that innovation requires willingness to act on what their creativity envisions.

The dynamic between comfort and innovation has an impact on our students, as well. Your struggling students might be too uncomfortable with the content to be creative learners. Setting aside time to fill the gaps in their understanding of lower-level material might get them to a point where they finally feel that they are capable of, and even excited about, taking on something newer.

At the other end of the spectrum, some of your high-performing students might be so comfortable with the ease of handling assignments that asking them to do something more creative might seem threatening. That is, if a student's grade is an "A" and the teacher introduces a different kind of assignment, that student might show some nervousness about the change. Letting them know you are confident they can handle the challenge might help.

Be honest with yourself about comfort's role in holding you back from trying something a little different. Thinking about what keeps you from acting on ideas might put you in a good position to help a student working with similar barriers.

Chapter 39

Compare Productively

You've likely seen this scenario play out before: A presenter shows some technique or a colleague talks about an activity that thrilled the students, and in the audience or from across the lunch table, you hear another teacher say, "I could never do that."

Maybe that doubting teacher was you.

Ahh, C.I.S., the devastating disease that from time to time keeps all of us from trying new things.

C.I.S., which I explored in some detail in *Making Your School Something Special*, is the horrible, soul-eroding malady of Comparative Inadequacy Syndrome. And it is very real, despite my having made up the name. It's that tendency to focus on what we can't do, and letting the thought forge a formidable barrier to trying something new.

That thought, I could never do that, comes from a confusion between replicating an activity and mimicking a style.

In 2016, at the wonderful edtech conference that is Fall CUE (fallcue.org), Dave Burgess of *Teach Like a Pirate* (daveburgess.com) fame kicked off the gathering in Napa, California. Burgess carries an Olympic level of enthusiasm and personality into what he does, and it is wonderful to watch. He goes to plenty of trouble to explain how one can adapt what he shows to a variety of classroom settings. However, his stage presence is so impressive that some in the audience can be intimidated at the thought that this is someone who is hired to do the same kind of work they do.

That isn't Burgess' fault, of course. It's the effect of a bad case of C.I.S. In reality, the reason he shares the ideas he does is because he believes every teacher can bring a higher level of enthusiasm to their classrooms. He isn't asking teachers to replicate what he does, but to follow his lead in bringing their personal passion to their teaching.

When seeing colleagues or presenters do really cool things, rather than assume you have to match their performance exactly, instead ask the following questions: What in that would work for me? What wouldn't I do and why? How would I approach the activity differently? What will I try?

And then try it! Meet up with colleagues later and discuss what you did, what worked, what didn't, and what you might do differently in the future. This reflection and brainstorming activity will help everyone develop confidence, which is one of the two active ingredients in the antidote to C.I.S.

The active ingredient that allows people to move past the discomfort of comparison and the barrier of comparative inadequacy? It's a simple idea, and has been shared in many ways. I word it for teachers this way: The only person to whom you ever need compare yourself is the you who you were yesterday.

It's true. Knowing—believing—that it's true can set you free from the shackles of that feeling of not being good enough to do new things.

No matter what you do and what your position, you can explore new ideas and develop new talents every day. In so doing, you'll learn you are capable of more than you may have ever believed.

Chapter 40

Stay Calm When an Argument Erupts

Living in California, I'm well aware that an earthquake can happen at any moment. Many in the state are somewhat prepared for it, in terms of having a stash of bottled water, canned food, a can opener, solar-powered lights, and some other things at the ready. You can never be fully prepared for the potential chaos of a disaster, of course, but if it does happen, you will be thankful for whatever preparations you have made.

Likewise, as a teacher (or as a professional in any field), it's important to be prepared for a few of the things that can happen without warning.

In my first decade of teaching, we were making the adjustment to the presence of the Internet. Should the school have a website? Should students have email addresses? These were the kind of technology questions we grappled with in the 1990s.

At some point, I began asking my students to have web-based e-mail addresses. The most common choices at the time were Hotmail and Yahoo. Several colleagues began doing the same kind of thing, as we figured that it was simpler than somehow being responsible for addresses the school assigned to the students.

During my prep period several months into one school year, I dropped by the classroom of a teacher who also was interested in tech things. I don't recall exactly what the papers I took to her were about, but I do know they had nothing to do with technology. She was teaching a class at the time, so I entered, waved, and put the papers on her desk so as to not interrupt any more than I already had.

No such luck.

She stopped her lesson and, with a raised voice, accused me of having taken over the e-mail effort. I didn't know what she meant, but I could see she was upset, and I began backing out of the room. She continued yelling at me (in front of the students) despite the fact that I had no idea what she was talking about. When I told her as much, she started describing the role she had for assigning student e-mail accounts, which I'd messed up by encouraging students to get web-based accounts.

Be ready to walk away when someone surprises you with a sudden argument.

I told her I was sorry, which prompted her to shout, "Don't be condescending to me!"

At this point, I was starting to get angry, as this was the first I'd heard of any e-mail program she was leading, and it was more than a little uncomfortable getting hammered in front of a bunch of students.

Fortunately, another colleague came in from the hall, and said, "Please. Let's discuss this in the office. Please."

We followed him into an office, another teacher stepped into the room with the students, and she continued to shout at me about e-mail. It was not what I would call an uplifting experience.

That argument, in terms of its sudden eruption and nasty negativity, is the kind of interpersonal earthquake that happens from time to time in schools.

Knowing that they happen means that you can at least be prepared to recognize such moments when they occur. As infuriating as any element of it might be, it's probably best simply to respond to any outbursts with, "Let's talk about this later," and walk away.

Earlier in the book, I suggested it is best to be comfortable with one's lack of omniscience when working with students. Similarly, we can't always know what may be stewing in the heart and mind of another member of the staff. It may be that I should have been aware of the concerns that led my colleague to explode at me, but for whatever reason, I wasn't.

Like I did in the story above, you may do something that upsets a colleague, and have no idea that you've done it. While you can hope that such things might get explored productively and in the right setting, you certainly can't count on it.

Be ready to walk away when someone surprises you with a sudden argument. You may be embarrassed or angry, and you may feel as if you've been wronged. If it happens at a time when students are present, it's critical to remember that you're still a teacher, and everything you say and do becomes a lesson.

I'm not proud of every moment I've had teaching, but the bad moments have helped me better understand that my environment is more complex than I knew. If this story has you more prepared to make a good choice when something bad suddenly happens, then what I experienced that day may have been worth it.

Chapter 41

Team Up from Time to Time

In most classrooms around the world, there is some number of students, and exactly one teacher. That's a shame because two teachers who work well together can make all manner of good things happen.

I've had the good fortune to work with several teachers from Japan over the past couple of decades. We were introduced to them through a company that connects Japanese people wanting to experience life overseas to schools willing to have them as assistant teachers.

Together, my colleagues and I planned lessons, teamed up to lead activities, and discussed what individual students might need. Our students benefited from having two teachers, each bringing a different set of experiences, talents, and interests to the table.

If I needed to be absent, I knew that the learning momentum would continue uninterrupted, as the students were in familiar hands. (It is rather difficult to find a substitute for a Japanese class who knows the language.)

My last year in California before my wife and I moved to Texas for a time was the year I shared the Silver Creek Thunderously Hip Japanese Language Program with Matt Hall. Matt may well be the coolest, most energetic teacher with whom I've ever had the opportunity to work. He has competed internationally as a juggler, and that just begins the list of interesting aspects of Matt's life.

He and I occasionally competed in class in a Japanese game called "*janken*" (a Japanese rock-paper-scissors arrangement) or have *kanji* contests with each other. The students loved watching two teachers go at it with the humor and intensity we displayed.

A decade later, as I was getting Next Vista going in the late 2000s, I taught part-time in order to feed my nonprofit habit. Two of those years, I shared a room with an English teacher named Lauren Uyeshiro, one of the most professional and dedicated teachers I've known. I would arrive during her last class, and she would stay in the room while I taught my one class.

Even with this arrangement, we had the chance to share ideas about the students in the two classes. It was fascinating seeing students day after day, watching to see how they responded to different activities, how they communicated their confusion, and what they would try to get away with. Later, Lauren and I would discuss what went well and didn't, laugh about moments when the students had surprised us with something clever, and encourage each other when something proved challenging.

You may have experienced something similar as one mentoring a new teacher, or as a new teacher being mentored by a talented master teacher. While those experiences are often designed to prepare the new teacher to be able to teach on his or her own successfully, I hope you have also had the chance to enjoy the kind of collaboration I've described above.

If you have never experienced working with someone directly, it's worth your time to give it a try. You may have a colleague at your school who is happy to visit your class for an activity, and who enjoys having you do the same. Sitting together and asking what you might be able to make happen is itself a good brainstorming exercise.

Consider the possibility of two teachers, each with classes of thirty students. How might it be different to have a class of sixty, but to have a partner with whom you know you can work successfully?

The professionally lonely nature of teaching is obvious when you can experience the fun of working with someone else dedicated to the same goals. Even though many educational systems may be built on a framework that assumes one teacher per class, you still have the ability to connect with a colleague at your school to see what you might make happen.

Why not try it?

Chapter 42

Ask for the Coolest Thing

Staff meetings probably aren't an item that makes the top of your coolest-things list.

So, what is at the top of your coolest-things list?

What have you seen or done or experienced lately that was exceptionally cool?

In *Making Your School Something Special*, I explored the idea of gathering, sharing, and building upon successes happening all around us every day. One way to make this happen is to ask for the cool things we are seeing around us. From an interpersonal perspective, asking colleagues about the coolest things they've seen lately can be a good way to establish a positive atmosphere. It's also an activity that contributes to a culture that is intentional about noticing and even creating cool scenarios. People will want to have an answer to your coolest-thing question.

In early 2016, I had the pleasure of visiting the headquarters of the Internet Archive. (If you didn't know there was such a thing, you should spend a little time at Archive.org. You'll be amazed at how many resources are available.) The best time to visit the physical headquarters is Friday at lunch. At that time, everyone in the building (workers and guests) heads downstairs for a buffet. They line up, get food, and the weekly meeting begins.

> If you knew you would be reporting to everyone else in your organization what you've been doing all week, wouldn't you be intentional about making sure you had something interesting to say?

The meeting leader (the founder, Brewster Kahle, was leader on the day I visited) then asks guests to introduce themselves. The brief introduction is followed by one of the most professionally interesting activities I've seen in a work setting. Every employee, from Kahle to the person who greets people at the front desk (not in that order), stands, one at a time, and describes what they have been working on that week. That is, everyone reports to everyone. Some folks would toss in other items, as well, regarding invitations to a hike in the redwoods or other activities that were more social than work related.

The result is that the employees are well aware of what's happening across the organization, they have a better knowledge of the people working outside their departments, and they are responsible for getting good things done.

That last part is the most fascinating to me. If you knew you would be reporting to everyone else in your organization what you've been doing all week, wouldn't you be intentional about making sure you had something interesting to say? I would! No one wants to say, "I haven't accomplished anything new."

How might this apply in our school settings? Well, what if teachers all met each week to talk about what the students were accomplishing in class? It would be clear when someone is simply talking about what gets covered, as opposed to what students are genuinely doing. While the average school schedule might or might not be well suited to allow this kind of flattened reporting structure, grade-level or departmental teams might be a good place to start.

The bottom line is that there are plenty of cool things happening in schools today. And if there isn't much interesting going on in your school, start making it happen! Share what you're noticing and what you're doing to contribute to the coolness, and ask your colleagues what they are seeing. Because when we share what we see, everyone can be inspired by and build upon the possibilities.

Chapter 43
Do What Inspires You

Before writing this chapter, I managed to get some serious inspiration.

I'll tell you about that inspiration, but first, it may be helpful to understand a little about how I write. I am at my most productive in San Francisco at a little hotel my wife and I have visited for years. I sit down and write for a while, taking breaks from time to time to walk around, get some food from the superb restaurants which seem to be everywhere, and take in the beautiful views of The City by the Bay.

On the afternoon I wrote this, I cranked out several pages of material the editors will mark up with wild abandon. (Admittedly, in the end, this makes it far better than what I first throw at them.) I then took a walk around City Hall, and passed by the box office for the San Francisco Symphony.

My musical choices typically reach back three to five decades, with very little from before that and minimal representation from what has been released since. As I see it, if you haven't seen Steve Lukather play a solo (look up "Rosanna" from a Toto live performance for a small piece of his genius), then you live an incomplete life.

However, the performance for the evening happened to be Beethoven's Ninth Symphony, which includes the wonderful "Ode to Joy." I considered the cost for a moment (I'm an educator who runs a charity, after all), made the decision to buy one of the last tickets available, and then there I was, listening to one of the greatest pieces of music ever written.

Beethoven's 9th, San Francisco Symphony
by Rushton Hurley (2017-02-03) (CC0)

One performance later, I walked out of that concert hall, energized and ready to write.

What I've written may prove compelling, and it may not. If the need in crafting a few paragraphs (or designing a learning activity) is to be pushed past thinking-of-doing into actually-doing, then my experience that night made it happen.

I've had a few people tell me, "I don't know what inspires me."

If that's you, then you know what you need to learn. Get started by talking with others about what inspires them. Have new experiences. Take a moment to consider what you might do if you were capable of anything.

The key to discovering what inspires you is to find what allows you to think differently, to see new options, and to create something in a way you haven't before. Is it listening to music? Taking a walk? Spending a few minutes with your cat or dog? Exercising? Sushi?

Whatever it is (or they are—there could be many things that inspire you), pursue those moments often and with intention. If you use the inspiration those moments elicit to create something new within what you do, you are likely to become the kind of teacher who inspires students to experience the true joy of learning.

The key to discovering what inspires you is to find what allows you to think differently, to see new options, and to create something in a way you haven't before.

Discussion Items for
Area 4: Collegiality and Professionalism

In your team meetings or brainstorming sessions with colleagues, use the following questions to explore possibilities for strengthening your work as part of the teaching team on your campus. As you come up with more questions like these that prove useful, please share them at tinyurl.com/MYTSS-suggestions.

1. What are the fun and cool ways you share ideas with colleagues? Do you make time regularly to brainstorm creatively with colleagues? If not, how soon can you start?

2. How do you share ideas with teachers from other schools? Are you connected with teachers in other countries? If not, explore Epals.com or a similar site to see what projects are offered, and discuss with a colleague whether this is something you can see yourself doing.

3. How do you tap into resources that are available for what you teach? How do you share what you've created with other teachers?

4. With a colleague, look over the videos at NextVista.org/videos and find items that prompt ideas for your teaching. What stands out and why?

5. What in your teaching practice have you done for a long time? Does it serve the purpose you originally imagined? How could you make it better?

6. Are there students who will fail your class? What is the evidence that you haven't given up on those who struggle? How convincing is that evidence?

7. What do you do that is so easy that you need almost no preparation to make it happen? Does that keep you from finding ways to make it more powerful for more students?

8. Have you looked at what colleagues do and tried bringing that into your own teaching? How do you find inspiration for trying something new?

9. Have you ever reacted too quickly and regretted what you said or did? What did you learn from the experience?

10. Which colleagues on your campus might be interested in working with you on a project in which you visit each other's classes to team teach? If you're up for giving it a try, when will you talk to one or more of those people about the possibility?

11. What's the coolest thing you've seen in the last month? What's the coolest answer to that question you've heard from a colleague?

12. Describe the moments when your best teaching ideas happen. How can you have more moments like that?

AREA 5

Logistics

Chapter 44

Know the Folks Who Make Your School Work

Great teachers and inspiring leaders may be the most obvious components of an exceptional school; however, there are many other people who make a school a welcoming and positive place for students. It is worth your time to get to know each one of them.

Let's start in the front office. The secretarial staff members are probably better informed about what is and what isn't working well at a school than almost anyone else in the building. They are often the first people with whom parents interact. They engage, on some level, with every teacher and leader in the building. And they aren't thanked enough for all the work they do.

Consider what it means that secretaries are often the face of the school to the parent community. If their professional interactions with teachers and leaders are negative, it's possible they will convey those bad feelings to parents—the people whose cooperation is most significant in helping a child succeed.

Likewise, their work may speed up or slow down based on how they feel about the people who are asking them to get something done. Sure, a true professional wouldn't let interpersonal concerns get in the way of making sure the school is the best it can be for everyone, but it is common to be less interested in helping those who are rude.

"You catch more flies with honey than you do with vinegar," as the saying tells us. Being nice to colleagues, no matter their professional positions, is a constructive approach. While that may sound obvious, it's surprising how many teachers don't take time to treat secretaries as full partners in the larger effort of the school to help students succeed.

One added thought regarding treating secretaries well has to do with their deadlines. Teachers get all sorts of notices from various offices, asking for information by a given time and date. There are normally good reasons for wanting that info by that time, and just as we wouldn't want our students to dismiss our requests, we shouldn't dismiss the requests of those working to keep our systems going— however annoying you may find the system to be. As mentioned above, you are more likely to receive their cheerful help if you have cheerfully responded to their requests.

From the front office, we'll head to the cafeteria. Do you know the names of the people who work in the cafeteria? You should. These are people who work hard for even less pay than you get as a teacher. Their work includes watching students in the full spectrum of their behavior, and they still come back each day to try and make sure everyone can show up in your classroom without the worries of hunger.

These workers know much more about the lives of the kids than one might guess, and can be integral partners in identifying issues early for students facing major challenges. They may be the first to notice signs of problems at home for students. The students on the free breakfast program may get their first kind greeting of the day from someone on the food-service team. They most certainly deserve your kindness.

Around the cafeteria, down the halls, and in your room, you'll find the janitors hard at work. The janitors are people I always made sure I got to know. If I needed a piece of equipment, I would go to a janitor before anyone else. They know where things are, and often could tell me the person I should approach for what I needed. Because they are in every part of the school, including the playground, janitors may also see interactions among students that could portend trouble for the larger community. Having good communication with them can head off such trouble.

In too many schools, the students treat janitors as people they can ignore. That's a pretty significant failing of the larger community, if one of the goals is for everyone to learn to be polite and respectful to each other. Teachers who convey the same lack of consciousness of (or even an observable disdain for) other adults at the school are teaching lessons that are counterproductive to helping children grow up to be honorable adults.

It's easy enough to say that others are important, but it's what you do that shows whether you believe it.

Plenty of other people deserve being mentioned as integral players in every school's success: parent volunteers, crosswalk guards, discipline and security officers, bus drivers, library aides, and maintenance people, to name a few. It's easy enough to say that others are important, but it's what you do that shows whether you believe it. Nurturing positive relationships with everyone at your school is simple:

Know their names. As with your students, make sure you know the name of every member of the school staff. Greet people by name when you see them and take time to talk about shared interests.

Say "thank you." Regularly thank folks for their work. The most common way to do this is to say something, but providing an occasional gift card, a bouquet of flowers, or a card signed by the team is a meaningful recognition of their efforts, as well. Take time in your team, department, or staff meetings to talk about the contributions of the non-teaching adults at the school. Celebrate their birthdays, too; it's a strong and personal way to convey that you see them as part of the team.

Involve them! These are people who, like you, are capable of making much more happen at a school with their own time. They may be willing (even eager) to help coach sports teams or work with you on a special evening event for parents who need extra services for their families. I worked at one school where one of the most popular clubs was one for which the lead advisor was a janitor on our staff.

Every adult who works at a school can help that school be something special for the students and their families. Know this, and always act accordingly.

Chapter 45

Know the Resources Available

What if you learned that one of your students had just become homeless? Do you know what services or arrangements are available to allow someone living on the streets to get a shower? If not, do you know who would know?

What if you notice that a student squints every time you put something on the board?

What would you do if a student had a seizure in your class?

Schools offer trainings to prepare teachers for emergencies and to recognize emotional or physical concerns with students, but often those trainings are attended (and delivered) with the sense that we're-only-doing-this-because-we're-required-to. Minimal reflection, though, makes it clear that the topics of health, homelessness, family challenges and abuse, and similar circumstances that affect students on a personal and academic level, are important. The question isn't, "Have you been trained?" Rather, it's, "Do you know what to do when a situation arises?"

Given the wealth of issues on the average teacher's plate, it's rare for anyone to suggest taking time to review training on issues like those listed above. Even if you and your colleagues can't devote a full meeting to retraining on such topics, you could have a time for a question of the week. Starting the meeting with a quick question on something everyone is supposed to know (CPR techniques, who handles reporting of abuse at home, etc.) can refresh everyone's memories. Perhaps you can put certain questions to your students between activities to make sure they know what to do when there's an emergency.

The incredible array of potential issues facing students and their families can seem overwhelming, so be intentional about becoming familiar with the services that are available in your school and community. You may want to compile a list of organizations (and contact information) for services including the following:

- Counseling for unplanned pregnancies
- Scholarships for students with special needs
- Special interests clubs
- City programs providing after-school activities
- Domestic violence shelters
- Assistance for those caught in human trafficking
- Drug counseling
- Food programs
- Anorexia/bulimia counseling
- Shelters for homeless families
- Career guidance opportunities
- College scholarship information
- Financial planning assistance
- Tutoring opportunities

Perhaps there are more issues today than in the past that teachers and school personnel have to address. Or maybe those issues are no longer being swept under the rug. Whatever the case, the good news is that there is more help available in the community than ever before. Services such as United Way's 2-1-1 (211.org, or call 2-1-1) can connect you with a wide variety of services based on your zip code, and are a good way to know what's available.

As you learn about the services available in your community, you'll be better equipped to help students, friends, and family members should the need arise.

Chapter 46

Be Prepared for Parents

I remember a time when parents came to the teacher to learn how they could work together to get a child to do better academically and even personally. In recent years, however, teachers have seen a rise in the number of combative parents who accuse them of incompetence when their children do poorly in school. The cherry on top of those conversations is the reminder that, "My taxes pay your salary!"

How you approach conversations with parents may well dictate the direction the discussion goes—and how helpful it proves for the student. Preparing in advance for any interaction with a parent can help ensure a productive, even positive, outcome.

First and foremost, be organized about what you say, when you say it, and to whom you say it. If you send a note home with a student to pass along to his or her parent, keep a copy for yourself. If the parent initiated the communication, make a note of when you spoke and what you discussed.

> ## How you approach conversations with parents may well dictate the direction the discussion goes—and how helpful it proves for the student.

It's easy enough to keep a record in an online document that you can access from any device. You might fill out a simple form you create to track date, time, person, student, and details. However you keep track of the information, you need to be able to search your document or spreadsheet so you can quickly reference previous conversations. In addition to specific issues with a student's performance, you might ask how a grandfather is doing when, in the last call, it was mentioned that he had been ill. Most parents greatly appreciate that you are kind enough to ask about the larger issues that may have an impact on a child's mood and studies.

In addition to recording parent conversations and notes home, you can also create a document recording summaries of all of your interactions with students and their parents or guardians. If you have a challenging moment with a child at school, make a note of it. If you have a phone call with a parent, make a note of it. If you receive an email with important items in it, you can copy them into the document.

This can all be done very quickly, and may save you immense headaches later. (If you are new to a school, your supervising administrator might be quite impressed that you go to the trouble to track things; a surprising number of teachers don't.)

All of this documentation is helpful for being able to speak in detail about a child's academic progress. When you can state exactly what a student is having difficulty with and can describe several strategies for how the parent might help the child do better, you set both parent and child up to be successful. You might also refer to resources available at the school if a parent is unable or unwilling to take a more active role.

Clearly, a parent's impression of you as the teacher will be much stronger if grades are objective and timely, and they can see a clearly articulated path for a student who needs to overcome a poor performance.

Parents and guardians can be your most powerful allies in helping a child succeed. How you communicate your expectations, reference past interactions and directions, and provide options will largely determine whether they embrace a supportive role or choose a more combative one.

Chapter 47

Choose between Permission and Forgiveness Wisely

"It's easier to beg for forgiveness than to ask for permission!"

I hear variations on the theme often, and it always makes me cringe. Usually those saying this are grinning or laughing and imply that whatever it is they did wouldn't have been approved had they asked permission. They did it anyway, and (as they seem to suggest) that's how they rebel against the system.

Indeed, bureaucratic morass can get in the way of doing things that should be and need to be done. There are also times when rules are in place for very good reasons, and not understanding that could get you fired for not having checked.

Beyond the importance of avoiding losing your job, your cooperation or defiance may make a profound impression on your students. Any teacher who suggests that one can pick and choose which rules to follow fails to understand that everything you do as a teacher can serve as a reason for a student to do something similar.

Would a teacher who uses the permission/forgiveness line above be okay with a student's choice to skip class? Why should the student bother asking permission when begging for forgiveness is easier?

Would a teacher who seeks forgiveness rather than permission be okay with a student using another student's work to complete his or her own? Why should the student bother asking permission when asking forgiveness is easier—if you happen to notice?

If a student explained to your boss that she heard you say forgiveness is easier than permission, would that go well for you?

Treating the issue honestly, we might identify a further flaw in the statement, and that has to do with timing. If one has utterly failed to plan for what needed to be done and get the necessary clearance to maintain accountability, yes, it's easier to go ahead and do something without permission. But you can avoid having to make that choice simply by preparing properly. Preparation is yet another sign that you are the professional the school and the students need you to be.

Being a good member of a team means learning what the processes are and following them. When you don't agree with a process, rather than putting yourself or your students at risk, engage in the kind of discussion that gets the process changed. In doing so, you prove yourself as a reliable member of the team, and that can open you up to opportunities for growth and advancement.

Chapter 48

Be Organized about Needs

Supportive administrators occasionally ask their teachers what they need. Teachers often respond with answers that look something like this:

"I need every kid to behave!"

"I need more hours in the day."

"I need all my students to get their homework done."

"I need a raise!"

What the principal, associate head of school, or visiting district person may have had in mind, though, was more like whiteboard markers.

Admittedly, when the person at Starbucks who just took my order for chai tea latte (no water) asks if I'd like anything else, I do toss out,

"More peace in the world," or "Civil political discourse." This usually elicits a smile and perhaps an apology that the needed button isn't on the register.

As educators, we have all sorts of little wants and needs. It might be a device for posting to a class social media account. It might be winter gloves for the kid who doesn't have any. It might be copy paper. It might be breakfast bars for the kid who shows up hungry.

Regardless, it makes sense to create a running list of wants and needs on a document that you can easily access from any device. Divide the list into two separate categories (not every want is a need) and add subcategories as needed (need fairly soon, need now, etc.). You might also add a space for notes about why each item is needed or wanted.

The idea is to know what you want and need, and to get good at explaining the value of what you ask for. Many teachers don't get much for their classrooms for the simple reason that they never ask. There are often people at the school or in the district, though, who are looking for good ways to direct funds associated with some budget or grant, and your wants or needs may be a perfect fit.

The more you know about such folks and their programs, and the better you get at explaining how what you want/need connects to what they do, the more you can get for your classroom.

Get good at explaining the value of what you ask for.

The timing of a request may be important, as well.

Early one summer after iMovie first came out, I decided it would be really cool to have some Macs in my classroom so students could do video projects.

I went to my principal and described my idea. Having these computers would allow them to learn to use video-editing tools to do their class projects. As I saw it, this could increase the quality of their work, if I made sure they kept focus on the content. If successful, this might inspire other teachers to try using (what was at the time) cutting-edge classroom technology. Finally, the students would be developing skills that could be helpful to them in a variety of fields.

I'd identified what we'd buy, from where, and why that would be the best vendor for the machines.

I put my reasons in front of him, and to my surprise, he told me that there were some extra funds related to technology needs, and that I should go see the guy in charge of that program. I did, and he approved the request—*woohoo*!

I asked when I could place the order, and he suggested we do so in August. When I pointed out that I'd hoped to have time to work with the computers during the summer in order to practice with iMovie and design the projects my students would do, he agreed with my logic and told me to go ahead and order them.

I did, and the computers came at the beginning of July. Two weeks later, a state budget issue prompted our district to put a freeze on all purchases.

That is to say, my timing was good. We got the Macs, I learned iMovie, and the students put some great material together.

Note that this went through because I had a compelling reason for the purchase I wanted the school to make. As you identify the things you want to have in your room, whether it's a laptop, a 3D printer, a new set of erasers, or anything else, fine-tune your reasons. Have colleagues look at the reasons and ask challenging questions so that you can clarify your reasons and answer any additional questions. You may need to be able to show how others are using the same tools and offer evidence of how those tools improve learning in those settings.

Once you're organized, then you can go after the resources to get what you want—and need.

Chapter 49

Foster Contacts with Supportive Organizations

In almost every community, there are people running programs that can benefit your students. These programs may well offer funding for projects you would like to pursue, and securing that funding may be as simple as asking for it.

There are also supportive organizations in the community which are capable of financing school programs with donations, providing scholarships, having members visit as guest speakers, and the like. Sometimes, no one has asked them for years (or ever).

Consider the role of service organizations such as Rotary, Kiwanis, Lions, Soroptimists, and other similar groups. These are clubs of people from a variety of professional backgrounds who get together regularly to share a meal and talk about projects they can support or initiate in the community. These clubs collect dues from their members, and often engage in fundraisers to support their community service efforts. More than that, the people who are part of these organizations enjoy being able to support good causes; they want to help and be actively involved in improving their community.

Many of these organizations give scholarships and awards to students in a variety of circumstances. In the area where I live, the Kiwanis club has a scholarship program for students who have overcome challenges and are trying to get into a community college or a vocational training program. The area Rotary clubs sponsor speech contests and give monetary awards to the students who reach the top of the club contest, and then again to those who are at the top regionally. Sometimes, no students enter the contests. What a missed opportunity for someone who needed to build some confidence!

Clubs like these or similar organizations are worth getting to know, as they tend to be filled with kind people who are willing to help. If you know someone who attends the club, make time to ask about the service projects they do, and if there is some semblance of a match with what you are trying to make happen, ask about the process for submitting a request. The worst you'll get is a "no," and you may find out about other opportunities you can try for later.

If you do get the chance to apply for some help, make sure that you have a clear and concise description of what you want to do and why, along with a budget with a reasonable level of detail. In addition, make sure you have researched the club and organization so that you can draw connections between your request and their mission.

And if you do receive some help, always, always, always send a thank-you note. Amazingly often, folks show up to receive a check, and the club never hears from them again. Needless to say, that limits one's chances of fostering a long-term relationship with the club. The more they know about what you do with their generosity, the better they feel about having provided some help, and the more likely that, should you need something else from them (a guest speaker at the school, for example), they will be interested in helping again.

Keep your school leadership informed about your requests, as well. They may have connections within the club that prove useful in optimizing your chances and in helping strengthen the relationship with the school.

If you do receive some help, always, always, always send a thank-you note.

(A friend of mine once earned a full class set of laptops, but didn't tell her principal until she got word they had been awarded. The principal was annoyed at not having been contacted earlier, and wouldn't let the IT team deploy the machines for an entire school year. While there's nothing impressive about the principal's actions, it's not a bad reminder that you sometimes run into egos that are big enough to get in the way of cool possibilities for students.)

The range of supporting organizations doesn't stop at service clubs, of course. There may be city government programs to support interesting projects. Local companies may have outreach programs that offer guest speakers, donated products or services, etc. A nearby training center, union office, or college or university may also have opportunities available.

You may also consider joining groups in your community. It can be energizing to work hand-in-hand with people from different professional backgrounds, and they are often fascinated by the stories we tell about our students. My Rotary club, the Rotary eClub of Silicon Valley, for example, is an online one (SiliconValleyRotary.com). The flexibility of attending the week's meeting at any time, day or night, is such that several educators have joined. The inspiration that comes from my Rotary connections generates all sorts of great things for my educational work. It is also a strong reminder that there are many people outside of education who care deeply about our creativity and innovation and what we can make happen for children.

The bottom line is that there are people who are willing to help you make some great things happen for students. It takes some legwork to figure out whether their interests will match yours. You'll also want to be aware of how your school's leaders might see reaching out to specific off-campus organizations. Like a good classroom activity or a good student project, planning and the courage to ask for help are key!

Chapter 50

Understand Donation Possibilities

With the development of online fundraising systems, there are plenty of possibilities for tapping into people's interest in helping make things happen for schools.

While there are multiple systems, I'll focus on DonorsChoose.org, as it's perhaps the best known, and, as of the time of writing, has funded over 875,000 projects in more than 73,000 schools. The ideas I'll share here can be applied to similar systems, and you are encouraged to work with one or two go-getter colleagues to explore as many different possibilities as you can.

Please note that DonorsChoose.org is a system that is specifically for projects for public schools, so if you are in a private religious or independent school, take these ideas and find something specific to your faith community or your geographic area that can support your school.

As we discussed a couple of chapters ago, you start with what you want and why. You'll typically need that information in order to complete the application offered by the donation system. One of the best components of a strong system like DonorsChoose.org is that it helps you understand the information that you must provide to make a compelling case for funding your project. Additionally, many of the projects teachers do are quite small. Working your way through a request for only $100 or so allows you to learn the system. What you can request initially is quite limited, but that can help you as you learn how their processes work.

I can hear the concerns now: "But I really want ten doodads, and that costs more than what a project can be for someone doing it for the first time. Do I need to find a different funding source?"

Nope. Write a project to see if you can get three or four of the doo-dads, and follow through with all the requirements, then do another project. That's a totally fine approach. The DonorsChoose.org folks are happy for people to learn to do this right, as that makes everyone happy (the donor, the teacher, and the DonorsChoose.org PR people).

A system like this also serves to remind you that when you're explaining why you want something, how you broadcast your interest is one thing. How others receive it is another.

How you broadcast your interest is one thing. How others receive it is another.

Make sure you use language that makes sense to the people who could fund you. In the case of DonorsChoose.org, funders are normal people who are putting a few dollars into the system to help something they think is cool. Weird educational language like, "differentiated instruction for the whole child," isn't likely to attract normal people to your side.

You should also explore the information on the site in as much detail as you can (start with DonorsChoose.org/about). There may be funding sources that are specific to your town or the subject you teach. The more you can reach out to those wanting to support what you do, the better off you are, obviously.

The best presentation on DonorsChoose.org I've ever seen is an hour-long EdTechTeam webinar by a former South Carolina teacher named Jed Dearybury (youtu.be/G7IUM38Aw8g). I'd recommend watching this webinar multiple times, as it is a gold mine of advice about promoting possibilities for your class.

He talks in detail about the importance of tapping your own networks, and telling everyone in your Facebook, Twitter, Instagram, etc. networks about what you're doing. If you ask a hundred people to give five dollars to support your students, you may just get that $500. Not everyone you ask will give, but many will, and some will give more than you ask for.

You can even set such programs in motion yourself. Here is an example of one my nonprofit did several years ago.

In 2012, I made a trip to a small town near Colima, Mexico, to work with a group of students in one of my favorite organizations, Project Amigo (ProjectAmigo.org). It's a sponsor-a-child program that helps students who are working really hard, but whose families don't have much of anything in terms of money. Project Amigo provides scholarships, homework help, and many other opportunities, and I've been a fan and supporter ever since I first learned about its work in May of 2006.

My 2012 trip was designed to help a group of their students learn to edit video, and with two buddies, we came up with the idea that we should try raising $1,500 to buy cameras and other equipment that we could teach them to use and leave with them so they could continue learning after we returned home.

On a Wednesday morning about six weeks before I was to leave, we posted a page on the Next Vista site with a PayPal button, outlining what we were planning to do and how folks could help. We contacted everyone we knew, asking each for five dollars, but also providing goodies for those contributing more. The $100 contributors, for example, would get their names in the credits of the videos the students created.

I figured if we raised $500, that would be a nice help to what we were spending on the project, and with six weeks, I felt the chances were pretty good.

Well.

By the next evening, we had the $1,500. People I hadn't seen in years kicked in anywhere from five to one hundred dollars, without any major donations skewing the cool outburst of support. By the time I flew to Mexico, we had almost $4,000, and we were able to get lots of extra equipment to support the students' efforts.

The thing to know is that, in the face of all kinds of nasty stuff you might endure from the nightly newscasts, despite the petty politics of folks in your system who should really go and make someone else miserable, and despite how draining it can be to put your all into teaching day in and day out, there are lots of quiet folks out there who are happy to cheer you on and support what you are making happen.

The world is a better place than it often seems, and what you do creates moments of encouragement, joy, and possibility for others. You never know when one of your students will take what they learn from you, and multiply it ten thousandfold.

Discussion Items for
Area 5: Logistics

In your team meetings or brainstorming sessions with colleagues, use the following questions to explore possibilities for strengthening your command of the logistical issues teachers face. As you come up with more questions like these that prove useful, please consider sharing them at tinyurl.com/MYTSS-suggestions.

1. What experiences with non-teaching, non-leadership staff at your school have resulted in better opportunities for you and/or your students? Which members of the larger school team do you still need to get to know?

2. What kinds of opportunities connected to people in your school or district do you need to learn more about to help specific students in your class?

3. What can you do to be better organized for parents when meeting to discuss a student's progress? What do you currently do to track communication with parents, and how can you improve it?

4. What kinds of activities have you held off trying because the bureaucratic requirements seemed onerous? Can you reach out to someone for help making new things happen?

5. What would make for a good addition to your classroom? Show colleagues what you have done to identify details related to wants or needs (items and cost, justification, secondary benefits), and get their feedback on how to improve what you have or whom to contact about them.

6. Which organizations have a history of, or have shown a readiness for, working to support efforts at your school? How can you develop contacts within organizations like these?

7. If your school is eligible for a DonorsChoose.org project, do some research on their site and describe to colleagues what you need to get one going. If your school is ineligible, what are the organizations that are willing to fund projects at your school?

The Final Bell

Saru mo ki kara ochiru.

This is a Japanese proverb, which in English is, "Even monkeys fall from trees."

The very best teachers are not those who make no mistakes. Instead, they are those whose mistakes become learning opportunities for them and for their students.

Perhaps the biggest mistake a teacher can make is to stop improving, and if you feel this is happening to you, then the good news is that you are one decision away from turning it around.

You care about teaching. I know you do because you've read this book to learn how to grow and improve as an educator. And because you care about teaching, I know you will devote time to trying new things. You will work to find what might help a struggling student. You will find ways to make what you do more interesting for your students and for yourself. And you will connect and collaborate with your colleagues who care enough to do these same things.

As you try, as you help, as you inspire, as you fail, and as you succeed, I hope you will share what you learn. Our learning moments are opportunities. In sharing them, we offer our colleagues around the world the chance to improve personally and professionally.

This book has given you fifty chapters' worth of advice to help you work toward being the best teacher you can be. Some of it will fit nicely with your personality and work patterns. Some will not.

Whatever it is that allows you to take a step in a better direction, it is my hope that it stokes or even reignites the passionate fire that brought you to teaching as a career.

So what might you do next? Well, I hope you'll consider reading *Making Your School Something Special* (edtech.team/school_special), which I wrote to help teachers and school leaders work together to foster and share successes in ways personally helpful to everyone. It dives into more detail about what makes learning activities effective and memorable, and what you and your colleagues can do to make those learning activities the stories that inspire the community.

Finally, I thank you for taking time to read what I've written. We share what we experience in order to help others, and the many teachers and leaders who have shared stories and ideas with me are to thank for whatever carries through as valuable for you.

I finish the newsletters I write for Next Vista for Learning with the same line every month, and I'll finish this book with the same line now:

May you inspire and be inspired—each and every day.

The Thanks

In my previous book, *Making Your School Something Special* (edtech. team/school_special), I filled several pages with thanks to people who have inspired me for many years. While I will not echo those thanks here, they hopefully know my profound appreciation for their dedication to their work and their encouragement of my efforts.

It is also good to have the chance to thank Chikao Tsuchiya, Yuko Sawa, and especially Aiko Shiokawa, who chose to come to the United States and spend a year of their lives working with a highly energetic and perhaps entertainingly nerdy Japanese language teacher who loves what learning that beautiful language can be for so many students on this side of the Pacific.

I give an extra shout-out to the amazing educators Kristen Swanson, Alice Keeler, Dennis Grice, and Diane Main for helping me understand the wonderful value of Edcamps and coffeeEDUs. Another shout-out goes to the teachers at Edcamp Silicon Valley who gathered at Palo Alto High School in February 2017: Amber Kraver, Dave Avery, Kristi Van, and the others who joined us that day for a great discussion on advice for teachers.

Another thank you goes to all those who provided advice on early drafts of this book, including Steve Hardy, Hadar Dohn, Karl

Lindgren-Streicher, Sumiko Clark, Emily Garrison, Yvonne Kwan, Aubrey Patterson, Theuns Opperman, and Dennis Grice.

Writing the last book also helped me appreciate the incredible value of having great editors. A thank you goes out to Erin Casey and her team, not just for helping my last book be much better than it would have been otherwise, but also for helping me become a better writer. I have described my experience with them as "energizingly humbling," and I hope what is in this book shows the improvement I feel is a result of their attention.

Final thanks go to my extended family; my cat Chiquita, whose purr can heal any malady; and especially my wife Tabitha, who is my best friend and the love of my life. As I see it, Tabitha's encouragement and affection make my life something truly special.

MORE BOOKS FROM EDTECHTEAM PRESS
EDTECHTEAM.COM/BOOKS

The HyperDoc Handbook
Digital Lesson Design Using Google Apps
By Lisa Highfill, Kelly Hilton, and Sarah Landis

The HyperDoc Handbook is a practical reference guide for all K–12 educators who want to transform their teaching into blended-learning environments. *The HyperDoc Handbook* is a bestselling book that strikes the perfect balance between pedagogy and how-to tips while also providing ready-to-use lesson plans to get you started with HyperDocs right away.

Innovate with iPad
Lessons to Transform Learning
By Karen Lirenman and Kristen Wideen

Written by two primary school teachers, this book provides a complete selection of clearly explained, engaging, open-ended lessons to change the way you use iPad with students at home or in the classroom. It features downloadable task cards, student-created examples, and extension ideas to use with your students. Whether you have access to one iPad for your entire class or one for each student, these lessons will help you transform learning in your classroom.

Assessment That Matters
Using Technology to Personalize Learning
By Kim Meldrum

In *Assessment That Matters*, Kim Meldrum explains the three types of assessment—assessment *as* learning, assessment *for* learning, and assessment *of* learning. Within her instruction on gathering rich assessment information, you'll find simple strategies and tips for using today's technology to allow students to demonstrate learning in creative and innovative ways.

The Space

A Guide for Educators

By Rebecca Louise Hare and Robert Dillon

The Space supports the conversation around revolution happening in education today concerning the reshaping of school spaces. This book goes well beyond the ideas for learning-space design that focuses on Pinterest-perfect classrooms and instead discusses real and practical ways to design learning spaces that support and drive learning.

A Learner's Paradise

How New Zealand Is Reimagining Education

By Richard Wells

What if teachers were truly trusted to run education? In *A Learner's Paradise,* Richard Wells outlines New Zealand's forward-thinking education system in which teachers are empowered to do exactly that. With no prescribed curriculum, teachers and students work together to create individualized learning plans—all the way through the high school level. Learn how New Zealand is reimagining education and setting an example for innovative educators, parents, and school districts to follow.

*Classroom Management in the Digital Age**

Effective Practices for Technology-Rich Learning Spaces

By Patrick Green and Heather Dowd

Classroom Management in the Digital Age helps guide and support teachers through the new landscape of device-rich classrooms. It provides practical strategies to novice and expert educators alike who want to maximize learning and minimize distraction. Learn how to keep up with the times while limiting time wasters and senseless screen-staring time.   **Also available in Spanish!*

The Google Apps Guidebook
Lessons, Activities, and Projects Created by Students for Teachers
By Kern Kelley and the Tech Sherpas

The Google Apps Guidebook is filled with great ideas for the classroom from the voice of the students themselves. Each chapter introduces an engaging project that teaches students (and teachers) how to use one of Google's powerful tools. Projects are differentiated for a variety of age ranges and can be adapted for most content areas.

Dive into Inquiry
Amplify Learning and Empower Student Voice
By Trevor MacKenzie

Dive into Inquiry beautifully marries the voice and choice of inquiry with the structure and support required to optimize learning. With *Dive into Inquiry*, you'll gain an understanding of how to best support your learners as they shift from a traditional learning model into the inquiry classroom, where student agency is fostered and celebrated each and every day.

Sketchnotes for Educators
100 Inspiring Illustrations for Lifelong Learners
By Sylvia Duckworth

Sketchnotes for Educators contains 100 of Sylvia Duckworth's most popular sketchnotes, with links to the original downloads that can be used in class or shared with colleagues. Interspersed throughout the book are reflections from Sylvia about what motivated her to create the drawings as well as commentary from many of the educators whose work inspired her sketchnotes.

Code in Every Class
How All Educators Can Teach Programming
By Kevin Brookhouser and Ria Megnin

In *Code in Every Class*, Kevin Brookhouser and Ria Megnin explain why computer science is critical to your students' future success. With lesson ideas and step-by-step instruction, they show you how to take tech education into your own hands and open a world of opportunities to your students. And here's the best news: You don't have to be a computer genius to teach the basics of coding.

Making Your School Something Special
Enhance Learning, Build Confidence, and Foster Success at Every Level
By Rushton Hurley

In *Making Your School Something Special*, educator and international speaker Rushton Hurley explores the mindsets, activities, and technology that make for great learning. You'll learn how to create strong learning activities and make your school a place where students and teachers alike want to be—because it's where they feel energized, inspired and special.

The Google Cardboard Book
Explore, Engage, and Educate with Virtual Reality
An EdTechTeam Collaboration

In *The Google Cardboard Book*, EdTechTeam trainers and leaders offer step-by-step instructions on how to use virtual reality technology in your classroom—no matter what subject you teach. You'll learn what tools you need (and how affordable they can be), which apps to start with, and how to view, capture, and share 360° videos and images.

Transforming Libraries
A Toolkit for Innovators, Makers, and Seekers
By Ron Starker

In the Digital Age, it's more important than ever for libraries to evolve into gathering points for collaboration, spaces for innovation, and places where authentic learning occurs. In *Transforming Libraries*, Ron Starker reveals ways to make libraries makerspaces, innovation centers, community commons, and learning design studios that engage multiple forms of intelligence.

The Google Infused Classroom
A Guidebook to Making Thinking Visible and Amplifying Student Voice
By Holly Clark and Tanya Avrith

This beautifully designed book offers guidance on using technology to design instruction that allows students to show their thinking, demonstrate their learning, and share their work (and voices!) with authentic audiences. *The Google Infused Classroom* will equip you to empower your students to use technology in meaningful ways that prepare them for the future.

Intention
Critical Creativity in the Classroom
By Amy Burvall and Dan Ryder

Inspiring and exploring creativity opens pathways for students to use creative expression to demonstrate content knowledge, critical thinking, and the problem solving that will serve them best no matter what their futures may bring. *Intention* offers a collection of ideas, activities, and reasons for bringing creativity to every lesson.

About The Author

Rushton Hurley is the founder and executive director of Next Vista for Learning (NextVista.org), which provides a free library of creative, educational videos by and for teachers and students. He has been a high school Japanese language teacher, a principal of an online school, a teacher trainer, an educational technology researcher, and a school reform consultant.

His graduate research at Stanford University included using speech recognition technology with beginning students of Japanese in computer-based role-playing scenarios for developing language skills. In the 1990s his work with teenagers at a high school in California led him to begin using Internet and video technologies to make learning more active, helping him reach students who had struggled under more traditional approaches.

In 2005, Rushton began speaking at conferences to help teachers working to discover what digital media and other technologies could do for their classes. In the last decade, Rushton has trained teachers and other professionals in North America, Europe, Asia, and Africa, presenting at regional, national, and international conferences. His fun and thoughtful talks center on the connection between engaging learning and useful, affordable technology, as well as professional perspectives in an ever-changing world.

CPSIA information can be obtained
at www.ICGtesting.com
Printed in the USA
FFOW01n1434030518
46459999-48385FF